Romans & Galatians

The Spirit of Jesus

A
MEDITATIVE
COMMENTARY
ON THE
NEW TESTAMENT

ROMANS & GALATIANS

THE SPIRIT OF JESUS

by Gary Holloway

LEAFWOOD
PUBLISHERS

ROMANS & GALATIANS: THE SPIRIT OF JESUS
Published by Leafwood Publishers

Copyright 2006 by Gary Holloway

ISBN 0-89112-502-7
Printed in the United States of America

Cover & interior design by Greg Jackson, Thinkpen Design

For information:
Leafwood Publishers
1648 Campus Court
Abilene, TX 79601
1-877-816-4455 (toll free)

Visit our website: www.leafwoodpublishers.com

06 07 08 09 10 / 7 6 5 4 3 2 1

To Earl Lavender, my dear friend, beloved brother, and colleague, who always encourages me in the Lord.

CONTENTS

INTRODUCTION

ROMANS

MEDITATIONS ON ROMANS

GALATIANS

MEDITATIONS ON GALATIANS

HEARING GOD IN SCRIPTURE

There are many commentaries, guides, and workbooks on the various books of the Bible. How is this series different? It is not intended to answer all your scholarly questions about the Bible, or even make you an expert in the details of Scripture. Instead, this series is designed to help you hear the voice of God for your everyday life. It is a guide to meditation on the Bible, meditation that will allow the Bible to transform you.

We read in many ways. We might scan the newspaper for information, read a map for location, read a novel for pleasure, or read a textbook to pass a test. These are all good ways to read, depending on our circumstances.

A young soldier far away from home who receives a letter from his wife reads in yet another way. He might scan the letter quickly at first for news and information. But his longing for his beloved causes him to read the letter again and again, hearing her sweet voice in every line. He slowly treasures each word of this precious letter.

BIBLE STUDY

So also, there are many good ways to read the Bible, depending on our circumstances. Bible study is absolutely necessary for our life with God. We rightly study the Bible for information. We ask, "Who wrote this?" "When was it written?" "Who were the original readers?" "How do these words apply to me?" More importantly, we want information about God. Who is he? What does he think of me? What does he want from me?

There is no substitute for this kind of close, dedicated Bible study. We must know what the Bible says to know our standing with God. We therefore read the Bible to discover true doctrine or teaching. But some in their emphasis on the authority and inspiration of the Bible have forgotten that Bible study is not an end in itself. We want to know God through Scripture. We want to have a relationship with the Teacher, not just the teachings.

Jesus tells some of God's people in his day, "You diligently study the Scriptures because you think that by them you possess eternal life. These are the Scriptures that testify about me, yet you refuse to come to me to have life" (John 5:39-40). He's not telling them to study their Bibles less, but he is reminding them of the deeper purpose of Bible study—to draw us to God through Jesus. Bible study is a means, not an end.

Yet the way many of us have learned to study the Bible may actually get in the way of hearing God. "Bible study" may sound a lot like schoolwork, and many of us were happy to get out of school. "Bible study" may call to mind pictures of intellectuals surrounded by books in Greek and Hebrew, pondering meanings too deep for ordinary people. The method of Bible study that has been popular for some time focuses on the strangeness of the Bible. It was written long ago, far away, and in languages we cannot read. There is a huge gap between us and the original readers of the Bible, a gap that can only be bridged by scholars, not by average folk.

There is some truth and some value in that "scholarly"method. It is true that the Bible was not written originally to us. Knowing ancient languages and customs can at times help us understand the Bible better. However, one unintended result of this approach is to make the Bible distant from the people of God. We may come to think that we can only hear God indirectly through Scripture, that his word must be filtered through scholars. We may even think that deep Bible study is a matter of mastering obscure information about the Bible.

MEDITATION

But we read the Bible for more than information. By studying it, we experience transformation, the mysterious process of God at work in us. Through his loving words, God is calling us to life with him. He is forming us into the image of his Son.

Reading the Bible is not like reading other books. We are not simply trying to learn information or master material. Instead, we want to stand under the authority of Scripture and let God master us. While we read the Bible, it reads us, opening the depths of our being to the overpowering love of God. "For the word of God is living and active. Sharper than any double-edged sword, it penetrates even to dividing soul and spirit, joints and marrow; it judges the thoughts and attitudes of the heart. Nothing in all creation is hidden from God's sight. Everything is uncovered and laid bare before the eyes of him to whom we must give account" (Hebrews 4:12-13).

Opening our hearts to the word of God is meditation. Although this way of reading the Bible may be new to some, it has a long heritage among God's people. The Psalmist joyously meditates on the words of God (Psalm 1:2; 39:3; 119:15, 23, 27, 48, 78, 97, 99, 148). Meditation is taking the words of Scripture to heart and letting them ask questions of us. It is slowing chewing over a text, listening closely, reading God's message of love to us over and over. This is not a simple, easy, or naïve reading of Scripture, but a process that takes time, dedication, and practice on our part.

There are many ways to meditate on the Bible. One is praying the Scriptures. Prayer and Bible study really cannot be separated. One way of praying the Bible is to make the words of a text your prayer. Obviously, the prayer texts of Scripture, especially the Psalms, lend themselves to this. "The Lord is my shepherd" has been the prayer of many hearts.

However, it is proper and helpful to turn the words of the Bible into prayers. Commands from God can become prayers. "You shall have no other gods before me" (Exodus 20:3) can be prayed, "Lord, keep me from anything that takes your place in my heart." Stories can be prayed. Jesus heals a man born blind (John 9), and so we pray, "Lord Jesus open my eyes to who you truly are." Even the promises of the Bible become prayers. "Never will I leave you; never will I forsake you" (Deuteronomy 31:6; Hebrews 13:5) becomes "God help me know that you promise that you are always with me and so live my life without fear."

Obviously, there are many helpful ways of hearing the voice of God in Scripture. Again, the purpose of Bible reading and study is not to know more about the Bible, much less to pride ourselves as experts on Scripture. Instead, we read to hear the voice of our Beloved. We listen for a word of God for us.

HOLY READING

This commentary reflects one ancient way of meditation and praying the Scriptures known as *lectio divina* or holy reading. This method assumes that God wants to speak to us directly in the Bible, that the passage we are reading is God's word to us right now. The writers of the New Testament read the Old Testament with this same conviction. They saw the words of the Bible speaking directly to their own situation. They read with humility and with prayer.

The first step along the way of holy reading is listening to the Bible. Choose a biblical text that is not too long. This commentary breaks Romans and Galatians into smaller sections. The purpose is to hear God's voice in your current situation, not to cover material or prepare lessons. Get into a comfortable position and maintain silence before God for several minutes. This prepares the heart to listen. Read slowly. Savor each word. Perhaps read aloud. Listen for a particular phrase that speaks to you. Ask God, "What are you trying to tell me today?"

The next step is to meditate on that particular phrase. That meditation may include slowly repeating the phrase that seems to be for you today. As you think deeply on it, you might even memorize it. Committing biblical passages to memory allows us to hold them in our hearts all day long. If you keep a journal, you might write the passage there. Let those words sink deeply into your heart.

Then pray those words back to God in your heart. Those words may call up visual images, smells, sounds, and feelings. Pay attention to what God is giving you in those words. Then respond in faith to what those words say to your heart. What do they call you to be and to do? Our humble response might take the form of praise, thanksgiving, joy, confession, or even cries of pain.

The final step in this "holy reading" is contemplation of God. The words from God that we receive deeply in our hearts lead us to him. Through these words, we experience union with the all-powerful God of love. Again, one should not separate Bible reading from prayer. The words of God in Scripture transport us into the very presence of God where we joyfully rest in his love.

What keeps reading the Bible this way from becoming merely our own desires read back into Scripture? How do we know it is God's voice we hear and not our own?

Two things. One is prayer. We are asking God to open our hearts, minds, and lives to him. We ask to hear his voice, not ours and not the voice of the world around us.

The second thing that keeps this from being an exercise in self-deception is to study the Bible in community. By praying over Scripture in a group, we hear God's word together. God speaks through the other members of our group. The wisdom he gives them keeps us from private, selfish, and unusual interpretations. They help us keep our own voices in check, as we desire to listen to God alone.

HOW TO USE THIS COMMENTARY

This commentary provides assistance in holy reading of the Bible. It gives structure to daily personal devotions, family meditation, small group Bible studies, and church classes.

DAILY DEVOTIONAL

Listening, meditation, prayer, contemplation. How does this commentary fit into this way of Bible study? Consider it as a conversation partner. We have taken a section of Scripture and then broken it down into four short daily readings. After listening, meditating, praying, and contemplating the passage for the day, use the questions suggested in the commentary to provoke deeper reflection. This provides a structure for a daily fifteen minute devotional four days a week. On the fifth day, read the entire passage, meditate, and then use the questions to reflect on the meaning of the whole. On day six, take our meditations on the passage as conversation with another who has prayed over the text.

If you want to begin daily Bible reading, but need guidance, this provides a Monday-Saturday experience that prepares the heart for worship and praise on Sunday. This structure also results in a communal reading of Scripture, instead of a private reading. Even if you use this commentary alone, you are not reading privately. God is at work in you and in the conversation you have with another (the author of the commentary) who has sought to hear God through this particular passage of the Bible.

FAMILY BIBLE STUDY

This commentary can also provide an arrangement for family Bible study. Many Christian parents want to lead their children in daily study, but don't know where to begin or how to structure their time. Using the six-day plan outlined above means the entire family can read, meditate, pray, and reflect on the shorter passages, using the questions provided. On day five, they can review the entire passage, and then on day six, read the meditations in the commentary to prompt reflection and discussion. God will bless our families beyond our imaginations through the prayerful study of his word.

WEEKLY GROUP STUDY

This commentary can also structure small group Bible study. Each member of the group should have meditated over the daily readings and questions for the five days preceding the group meeting, using the method outlined above. The day before the group meeting, each member should read and reflect on the meditations in the commentary on that passage. You then can meet once a week to hear God's word together. In that group meeting, the method of holy reading would look something like this:

Listening
    1) Five minutes of silence.
    2) Slow reading of the biblical passage for that week.
    3) A minute of silent meditation on the passage.

4) Briefly share with the group the word or phrase that struck you.

Personal Message
   5) A second reading of the same passage.
   6) A minute of silence.
   7) Where does this touch your life today?
   8) Responses: I hear, I see, etc.

Life Response
   9) Brief silence.
   10) What does God want you to do today in light of this word?

Group Prayer
   11) Have each member of the group pray aloud for the person on
       his or her left, asking God to bless the word he has given them.

   The procedure suggested here can be used in churches or in
neighborhood Bible studies. Church members would use the daily
readings Monday-Friday in their daily devotionals. This commentary
intentionally provides no readings on the sixth day, so that we can
spend Saturdays as a time of rest, not rest from Bible study, but a time
to let God's word quietly work its way deep into our hearts. Sunday
during Bible school or in home meetings, the group would meet to
experience the weekly readings together, using the group method
described above. It might be that the sermon for each Sunday could
be on the passage for that week.
   There are churches that have used this structure to great advantage. In the hallways of those church buildings, the talk is not of the
local football team or the weather, but of the shared experience of the
Word of God for that week.
   And that is the purpose of our personal and communal study, to
hear the voice of God, our loving Father who wants us to love him in

return. He deeply desires a personal relationship with us. Father, Son, and Spirit make a home inside us (see John 14:16-17, 23). Our loving God speaks to his children! But we must listen for his voice. That listening is not a matter of gritting our teeth and trying harder to hear. Instead, it is part of our entire life with God. That is what Bible study is all about.

Through daily personal prayer and meditation on God's word and through a communal reading of Scripture, our most important conversation partner, the Holy Spirit, will do his mysterious and marvelous work. Among other things, the Spirit pours God's love into our hearts (Romans 5:5), bears witness to our spirits that we are God's children (Romans 8:16), intercedes for us with God (Romans 8:26), and enlightens us as to God's will (Ephesians 1:17).

So this is an invitation to personal daily Bible study, to praying the Scriptures, to sharing with fellow believers, to hear the voice of God. God will bless us, our families, our churches, and his world if we take the time to be still, listen, and do his word.

THE SPIRITUALITY OF ROMANS

Romans is an unusual letter of Paul in many ways. He writes to a church he did not plant, one he had not even visited. He writes to get that church's support for his mission efforts to Spain (Romans 15:23-24). What do you say to a church you have not visited? Paul takes the opportunity to describe the message he proclaims everywhere he goes, the good news of Jesus Christ. That's why Romans is the most theological of Paul's letters, and why it has (unfortunately) engendered the most controversy.

But the point of Romans is not to answer all our theological questions or to provide fodder for disagreement. Quite the opposite.

Romans is a deeply spiritual book, intended to unite God's people in the story of Jesus. That's why the book of Romans has radically changed the lives of countless Christians, including historic leaders like Augustine, Martin Luther, and Karl Barth. However, one does not have to be a famous theologian to be moved by Paul's heartfelt discussion of themes at the heart of the good news of Jesus-sin, grace, love, and the work of the Holy Spirit. Indeed, although the Spirit is prominent in all New Testament writings, the spirituality of Romans is the story of the work of the Spirit in our lives.

Gospel

Paul begins and ends his letter with a discussion of the gospel-the good news of what God has done in Christ. Paul is an apostle of the gospel, which although "news" is actually a continuation of God's work through the prophets (Romans 1:1-2). He is eager to proclaim that gospel in Rome, because it is powerful to all who believe (Romans 1:15-17). It is Paul's priestly duty and his ambition to preach the gospel where it had not been heard (Romans 15:16-20).

Although Paul rarely uses the word gospel in the middle of his letter, that's what the letter is about. Paul wants the Romans to assist him in his missionary journeys, so they need to understand the message he preaches. More importantly, God speaks to us through the words of Romans, reminding us of the power of the story of Jesus in our lives today. That good news is still the message we live and we proclaim.

Sin

However, before it gets to the good news, Romans gives the bad news first. The bad news is that we all sin and fall short of God's glory (Romans 3:23). Surely, that is not news. We know we are sinners. But we might think we are not as bad sinners as others. We don't murder, abuse children, or worship idols. We know we sin, but at least we are trying not to. Romans makes it clear that comparing ourselves to other sinners gives us no place to boast before God. We still fall short of what God made us to be.

GRACE

The bad news leads to good news. All sin, but all "are justified freely by his grace through the redemption that came by Christ Jesus" (Romans 3:24). Through grace, all our sins are forgiven; "where sin increased, grace increased all the more…" (Romans 5:20). By trusting the gracious promises of God, we have peace, freedom, and joy. By grace, the death that came from Adam is undone in Christ (Romans 5:12-19). By grace, we have died with Christ and been raised to live a new life (Romans 6). By grace, we are given different gifts for the sake of others (Romans 12:3-8).

SPIRIT

By grace, we are also given the Holy Spirit, the Spirit of Christ. In Christ, there is no condemnation because the law of the Spirit sets us free from the law of sin and death (Romans 8:1-2). The Spirit controls us and frees us from slavery to sin (Romans 8:4-10). Through the Spirit, our bodies will be raised from the dead (Romans 8:11). The Spirit confirms that we are beloved children of God, and we can call him, "Abba," Father (Romans 8:15-17). The Spirit helps us in our weaknesses, interceding for us in prayer (Romans 8:26-27).

Spirituality in Romans (and in the rest of the Bible) is thus the work of the Holy Spirit in us. While we do not always understand how the Spirit works in us (God's ways are beyond us, see Romans 11:33-36), we trust that he does. What's more, we open our hearts and lives to him, so he can control all of us, even our bodies (Romans 12:1-2).

Love

"God has poured out his love into our hearts by the Holy Spirit, whom he has given us" (Romans 5:5). Therefore, nothing can separate us from the love of God through Christ (Romans 8:28-39). As those who receive God's love, we are called to show his love to others, especially our fellow Christians (Romans 12:9-10, 13:8-10). This means giving up our cherished beliefs and practices for the sake of brothers and sisters who might be harmed spiritually by them (Romans 14). It even means loving our enemies by doing good to them and leaving vengeance to God (Romans 12:14-21).

Good News Spirituality

So as we read and meditate on Romans, we should let the good news of Jesus sink deep within our hearts. Let us read in full awareness that we are sinners, but sinners with a Savior. Let us whole-heartedly embrace the grace of God for us and for our neighbors. Let us open our lives to the powerful leading of the Spirit. And, fully convinced that nothing can separate us from God's love, let us show that love to all around us, especially those hard to love. To read Romans this way is to do more than simply know the gospel. It is to have the gospel live in us.

GOOD NEWS

(ROMANS 1:1-17)

DAY ONE READING AND QUESTIONS

¹Paul, a servant of Christ Jesus, called to be an apostle and set apart for the gospel of God— ²the gospel he promised beforehand through his prophets in the Holy Scriptures ³regarding his Son, who as to his human nature was a descendant of David, ⁴and who through the Spirit of holiness was declared with power to be the Son of God by his resurrection from the dead: Jesus Christ our Lord. ⁵Through him and for his name's sake, we received grace and apostleship to call people from among all the Gentiles to the obedience that comes from faith.

1. Ancient letters began with three parts—"from," "to," and "greetings." In Romans 1:1-7, which of these three parts is the longest? Why?

2. What two terms does Paul use to describe himself? What do those two words mean? Why does he introduce himself this way?

3. In describing himself to the Romans, Paul actually talks more about someone else. Who? Why?

DAY TWO READING AND QUESTIONS

⁶And you also are among those who are called to belong to Jesus Christ.

⁷To all in Rome who are loved by God and called to be saints:
Grace and peace to you from God our Father and from the Lord Jesus Christ.

1. What does it mean to be called? How are we called as Christians? Who calls us? To what are we called?

2. What does "saint" imply to you? Are all Christians saints or only those especially holy? What is the relationship between love and being saints?

3. What does "grace" mean to you? How about "peace"? What words do we use to greet fellow Christians?

DAY THREE READING AND QUESTIONS

⁸First, I thank my God through Jesus Christ for all of you, because your faith is being reported all over the world. ⁹God, whom I serve with my whole heart in preaching the gospel of his Son, is my witness how constantly I remember you ¹⁰in my prayers at all times; and I pray that now at last by God's will the way may be opened for me to come to you.

¹¹I long to see you so that I may impart to you some spiritual gift to make you strong— ¹²that is, that you and I may be mutually encouraged by each other's faith. ¹³I do not want you to be unaware, brothers, that I planned many times to come to you (but have been

prevented from doing so until now) in order that I might have a harvest among you, just as I have had among the other Gentiles.

[14]I am obligated both to Greeks and non-Greeks, both to the wise and the foolish. [15]That is why I am so eager to preach the gospel also to you who are at Rome.

1. *What is Paul's prayer for the Romans? What does he want God to let him do? Why? How do we pray for others? Do we ask only for physical blessings for them or spiritual ones as well?*

2. *What spiritual gift does Paul want to impart to the Romans? What does this say about Paul and his ministry?*

3. *What does Paul mean by being a debtor to certain people? What does he owe them? What do we owe people today?*

DAY FOUR READING AND QUESTIONS

[16]I am not ashamed of the gospel, because it is the power of God for the salvation of everyone who believes: first for the Jew, then for the Gentile. [17]For in the gospel a righteousness from God is revealed, a righteousness that is by faith from first to last, just as it is written: "the righteous will live by faith."

1. *What exactly is the gospel (good news)? How would you briefly describe it to someone who had never heard it?*

2. *Why is the gospel first for the Jew, then for the Gentile? Is this fair?*

3. *What does "righteousness" mean? What other words describe "righteousness"?*

Day Five Reading and Questions

Go back and read the entire passage.

1. *After reading these verses, why do you think Paul wrote Romans?*

2. *How had the good news affected Paul's life? The Romans' life? Your life?*

3. *Do we really believe the gospel has power? What kind of power? Are we ashamed of that power? Do we sometimes act like we are? How?*

MEDITATION ON ROMANS 1:1-17

Good news. We live for good news, long for good news, can't wait to share good news.

But this is the greatest news of all, the good news of the gospel. We all know that good news—that God so loved the world, that Jesus died for our sins, that death has been defeated by the resurrection. To many of us it is an old, old, story.

So why aren't we excited by the good news? Why aren't we eager to tell it to others? Perhaps because it is so old. Perhaps because the good news has often been twisted into bad news. Into legalism: "You must keep all God's rules to receive the good news." Into judgment: "You are wrong and will burn in hell if you do not obey the gospel." Into violence and oppression: "Since you do not follow Christianity, we must destroy you."

But perhaps our lack of excitement is due to another misunderstanding. We think the gospel is just a story to believe instead of our story, the story in which we live. Not so Paul. Certainly, he believed the story of Jesus, but that story had taken hold of him and changed him completely. He was now a slave of Christ Jesus. He was set apart for the gospel. He was indebted to Jew and Gentile, that is, he owed them the good news of Jesus.

Paul knows the power of the good news. Power to save. Power to make us right. Power to change everything.

Do we know that power? Paul writes to the Romans and to us to share the power of the good news.

"God of love, may we this day know the power of the good news, the power that makes us saints, calls us to belong to Jesus, and obligates us to others."

BAD NEWS
(ROMANS 1:18-2:29)

Day One Reading and Questions

¹⁸The wrath of God is being revealed from heaven against all the godlessness and wickedness of men who suppress the truth by their wickedness, ¹⁹since what may be known about God is plain to them, because God has made it plain to them. ²⁰For since the creation of the world God's invisible qualities—his eternal power and divine nature—have been clearly seen, being understood from what has been made, so that men are without excuse.

1. *What is your first reaction to "the wrath of God" (1:18)? Is God angry? What makes him angry? How does that square with his love? Would it be better if God were not angry at sin?*

2. *Are God's qualities plain to everyone? Then why* (ps. 19) *do some deny that there is a God? Do people become atheists because they intellectually do not believe in God or are there other reasons?*

3. *Do those who have never heard of God still have an obligation to believe in him? If so, how would they show they believe in God? How do people show they do not believe in God?*

Day Two Reading and Questions

[21]For although they knew God, they neither glorified him as God nor gave thanks to him, but their thinking became futile and their foolish hearts were darkened. [22]Although they claimed to be wise, they became fools [23]and exchanged the glory of the immortal God for images made to look like mortal man and birds and animals and reptiles.

[24]Therefore God gave them over in the sinful desires of their hearts to sexual impurity for the degrading of their bodies with one another. [25]They exchanged the truth of God for a lie, and worshiped and served created things rather than the Creator—who is forever praised. Amen.

[26]Because of this, God gave them over to shameful lusts. Even their women exchanged natural relations for unnatural ones. [27]In the same way the men also abandoned natural relations with women and were inflamed with lust for one another. Men committed indecent acts with other men, and received in themselves the due penalty for their perversion.

[28]Furthermore, since they did not think it worthwhile to retain the knowledge of God, he gave them over to a depraved mind, to do what ought not to be done. [29]They have become filled with every kind of wickedness, evil, greed and depravity. They are full of envy, murder, strife, deceit and malice. They are gossips, [30]slanderers, God-haters, insolent, arrogant and boastful; they invent ways of doing evil; they disobey their parents; [31]they are senseless, faithless, heartless, ruthless. [32]Although they know God's righteous decree that those who do such things deserve death, they not only continue to do these very things but also approve of those who practice them.

1. What is the basic sin condemned in this passage? What should humans know that they refuse to know?

2. Why is homosexuality singled out in this passage? How does it relate to failing to recognize God?   1 Cor 6:9

3. What other sins are mentioned here? Why does Paul discuss sin so soon after talking about the gospel?

DAY THREE READING AND QUESTIONS

[1]You, therefore, have no excuse, you who pass judgment on someone else, for at whatever point you judge the other, you are condemning yourself, because you who pass judgment do the same things. [2]Now we know that God's judgment against those who do such things is based on truth. [3]So when you, a mere man, pass judgment on them and yet do the same things, do you think you will escape God's judgment? [4]Or do you show contempt for the riches of his kindness, tolerance and patience, not realizing that God's kindness leads you toward repentance?

[5]But because of your stubbornness and your unrepentant heart, you are storing up wrath against yourself for the day of God's wrath, when his righteous judgment will be revealed. [6]God "will give to each person according to what he has done." [7]To those who by persistence in doing good seek glory, honor and immortality, he will give eternal life. [8]But for those who are self-seeking and who reject the truth and follow evil, there will be wrath and anger. [9]There will be trouble and distress for every human being who does evil: first for the Jew, then for the Gentile; [10]but glory, honor and peace for everyone who does good: first for the Jew, then for the Gentile. [11]For God does not show favoritism.

[12]All who sin apart from the law will also perish apart from the law, and all who sin under the law will be judged by the law. [13]For it is not those who hear the law who are righteous in God's sight, but it is

those who obey the law who will be declared righteous. [14](Indeed, when Gentiles, who do not have the law, do by nature things required by the law, they are a law for themselves, even though they do not have the law, [15]since they show that the requirements of the law are written on their hearts, their consciences also bearing witness, and their thoughts now accusing, now even defending them.) [16]This will take place on the day when God will judge men's secrets through Jesus Christ, as my gospel declares.

1. *If we judge others for sins we ourselves commit, what does that make us?*

2. *What is God's kindness intended to produce? Does sin have to separate us from God?*

3. *How will we be judged by God?*

DAY FOUR READING AND QUESTIONS

[17]Now you, if you call yourself a Jew; if you rely on the law and brag about your relationship to God; [18]if you know his will and approve of what is superior because you are instructed by the law; [19]if you are convinced that you are a guide for the blind, a light for those who are in the dark, [20]an instructor of the foolish, a teacher of infants, because you have in the law the embodiment of knowledge and truth— [21]you, then, who teach others, do you not teach yourself? You who preach against stealing, do you steal? [22]You who say that people should not commit adultery, do you commit adultery? You who abhor idols, do you rob temples? [23]You who brag about the law, do you dishonor God by breaking the law? [24]As it is written: "God's name is blasphemed among the Gentiles because of you."

[25]Circumcision has value if you observe the law, but if you break the law, you have become as though you had not been circumcised. [26]If those who are not circumcised keep the law's requirements, will they not be regarded as though they were circumcised? [27]The one who is not circumcised physically and yet obeys the law will condemn you who, even though you have the written code and circumcision, are a lawbreaker.

[28]A man is not a Jew if he is only one outwardly, nor is circumcision merely outward and physical. [29]No, a man is a Jew if he is one inwardly; and circumcision is circumcision of the heart, by the Spirit, not by the written code. Such a man's praise is not from men, but from God.

1. *Is it enough to know the law of God? What else must one do?*

2. *What is the significance of circumcision? How can those who are not circumcised be regarded as circumcised?*

3. *What does it mean to be a Jew inwardly? Why would one want to be a Jew?*

DAY FIVE READING AND QUESTIONS

Go back and read the entire passage.

1. *Is this section meant to frighten us into obeying God? If not, why does Paul talk about judgment?*

2. *Can we always obey God? Are we all doomed to wrath and anger?*

3. *Why does Paul say trouble and distress will come first to Jew, then Gentile? What else came first to Jews, then Gentiles?*

MEDITATION ON ROMANS 1:18-2:29

The wrath of God.

I really don't want to hear about it. It reminds me of all the "hell-fire and brimstone" sermons of my youth. It reminds me of all the reasons why many do not accept the Christian story as good news. "If that's the kind of God you worship," they say, "I don't want any part of it."

The wrath of God. Why does Paul spoil a beautiful letter on the good news of Jesus, a letter of grace and love, by talking about God's anger? Because he understands that the wrath of God against wickedness (a little-used word in our day) is an expression of God's love.

If that sounds strange, think about human relationships. Are parents who never correct their children good fathers and mothers? If the boss never checks up on our work does that make her a good supervisor? If criminals are never rehabilitated, is that a good thing? Instead, wouldn't we say that a parent, a boss, or a society that never disapproves the actions of others really does not care about them?

Unconditional love does not mean we ignore the harmful acts of those we love. Instead, it requires that we gently correct them. That's what the wrath of God is all about. God is not in a bad mood. He is not an angry, out-of-control, unpredictable Father who punishes only when he feels like it. No. Paul makes it clear he is a God who loves all his people, Jew and Gentile alike. He loves them enough to make his nature known to them. He loves them enough to want a relationship with him. He loves them enough that if they reject him and his ways, he gives them the freedom to sink into selfishness, shame, and violence. God even loves the hypocrites who condemn others for the very sins they themselves commit. He even loves them enough to have consequences for that rejection, consequences designed to turn them back to God, the source of life.

So is the wrath of God good news? Yes. It is the strong side of God's love. It shows how much God wants us. He wants more than mere outward obedience. He wants our hearts.

"Father, may we love you enough to fear your disapproval. May your anger lead us to turn to you, knowing that we can rely on your kindness."

Jane Sublett - cancer on spine
Linda Gilliam - loss of husband
Laura's F-in-law - cancer is contained
Amy - in hospital
Pam W. - in nursing home, her kids

ALL SIN, ALL JUSTIFIED

(ROMANS 3:1-31)

DAY ONE READING AND QUESTIONS

[1]What advantage, then, is there in being a Jew, or what value is there in circumcision? [2]Much in every way! First of all, they have been entrusted with the very words of God.

[3]What if some did not have faith? Will their lack of faith nullify God's faithfulness? [4]Not at all! Let God be true, and every man a liar. As it is written:

"So that you may be proved right when you speak
  and prevail when you judge."

[5]But if our unrighteousness brings out God's righteousness more clearly, what shall we say? That God is unjust in bringing his wrath on us? (I am using a human argument.) [6]Certainly not! If that were so, how could God judge the world? [7]Someone might argue, "If my falsehood enhances God's truthfulness and so increases his glory, why am I still condemned as a sinner?" [8]Why not say—as we are being slanderously reported as saying and as some claim that we say—"Let us do evil that good may result"? Their condemnation is deserved.

1. *What advantage do Jews have? Do they still have an advantage over Gentiles? In what way?*

2. *Do we make God look better (by contrast) when we sin? If our sin*

gives God a chance to forgive us and be gracious, isn't that a good thing? If so, doesn't our sin glorify God?

3. Is God to blame for our unfaithfulness? How do some try to blame him?

DAY TWO READING AND QUESTIONS

[9]What shall we conclude then? Are we any better? Not at all! We have already made the charge that Jews and Gentiles alike are all under sin. [10]As it is written:

"There is no one righteous, not even one;
　　[11]there is no one who understands,
　　no one who seeks God.
　[12]All have turned away,
　　they have together become worthless;
　there is no one who does good,
　　not even one."
　[13]"Their throats are open graves;
　　their tongues practice deceit."
　"The poison of vipers is on their lips."
　　[14]"Their mouths are full of cursing and bitterness."
　[15]"Their feet are swift to shed blood;
　　[16]ruin and misery mark their ways,
　[17]and the way of peace they do not know."
　　[18]"There is no fear of God before their eyes."

[19]Now we know that whatever the law says, it says to those who are under the law, so that every mouth may be silenced and the whole world held accountable to God. [20]Therefore no one will be declared righteous in his sight by observing the law; rather, through the law we become conscious of sin.

1. Is it true that no one is righteous? Are humans really that bad? Why?

2. How does the law silence every mouth and hold all people account-able?

3. How does the law make us conscious of sin? Is it good to know we are sinners?

DAY THREE READING AND QUESTIONS

[21]But now a righteousness from God, apart from law, has been made known, to which the Law and the Prophets testify. [22]This righteousness from God comes through faith in Jesus Christ to all who believe. There is no difference, [23]for all have sinned and fall short of the glory of God, [24]and are justified freely by his grace through the redemption that came by Christ Jesus. [25]God presented him as a sacrifice of atonement, through faith in his blood. He did this to demonstrate his justice, because in his forbearance he had left the sins committed beforehand unpunished—[26]he did it to demonstrate his justice at the present time, so as to be just and the one who justifies those who have faith in Jesus.

1. How are we made right with God apart from the Law? Who does this?

2. How is Jesus a sacrifice of atonement? Why do we need such a sacrifice? Can't God just forgive us without such a sacrifice?

3. How can God forgive our sins and still be just and fair?

Day Four Reading and Questions

[27]Where, then, is boasting? It is excluded. On what principle? On that of observing the law? No, but on that of faith. [28]For we maintain that a man is justified by faith apart from observing the law. [29]Is God the God of Jews only? Is he not the God of Gentiles too? Yes, of Gentiles too, [30]since there is only one God, who will justify the circumcised by faith and the uncircumcised through that same faith. [31]Do we, then, nullify the law by this faith? Not at all! Rather, we uphold the law.

1. *Why does our forgiveness exclude boasting? What do some religious people brag about? Should they?*

2. *What does it mean to be justified by faith apart from observing the law? Does this mean we can ignore the commands of God?*

3. *How are Jews and Gentiles alike in this passage?*

Day Five Reading and Questions

Go back and read the entire passage.

1. *Are people basically good or basically evil? What does this passage say? Does that square with your own experience?*

2. *In Romans 3:22-24, Paul says all have sinned and all are justified. Is everyone justified by God's grace? How? Does this mean everyone will be saved?*

3. *What does the word "faith" mean in this passage?*

MEDITATION ON ROMANS 3:1-31

Aren't most people good? Are we really that sinful or do Christians like to make the world seem worse than it really is?

I must admit that most of the time, I think people are basically good. That's because I live around nice, suburban, law-abiding citizens like me. But if you read the paper or watch the news, you know better. There is real evil in the world. Terrorists target the innocent. Corporate leaders cheat thousands out of their savings. Parents abuse and murder their own children.

Of course, we know there is evil "out there." We know "they" are evil.

"Are we any better?" This is the question Paul asks. Our first response might be, "Of course we are!" We do not bomb or cheat or murder. We are the good people.

Are we? As good as we may be, do we not still fall short of what God intends? Do we condemn others for their sins while excusing our own? All sin. All fall short. Think of the Olympic high jump competition. The bar is set at 2.3 meters to qualify. Suppose you jump 2.2 meters while most of the rest of the field only jump 2.0. What is the result? All fail to qualify. You can't feel superior to others if none of you made it over the bar.

So it is with us. We must admit that sin is not "out there" but in here, in the depths of our hearts. If we can admit it, if we see ourselves as we really are, then there is good news. All fall short. All "are justified freely by his grace through the redemption that came by Christ Jesus." We cannot jump over the bar. Jesus did. If we trust him, we clear the bar easily.

And we cannot brag about it. We cannot feel proud that we are a little superior to others. We can only thank God for his marvelous gift.

"Father, forgive our pride and our attempts to justify ourselves. May we trust the good news of Jesus, that through him we are right with you."

TRUST GOD'S PROMISE
(ROMANS 4:1-25)

DAY ONE READING AND QUESTIONS

[1]What then shall we say that Abraham, our forefather, discovered in this matter? [2]If, in fact, Abraham was justified by works, he had something to boast about—but not before God. [3]What does the Scripture say? "Abraham believed God, and it was credited to him as righteousness."

[4]Now when a man works, his wages are not credited to him as a gift, but as an obligation. [5]However, to the man who does not work but trusts God who justifies the wicked, his faith is credited as righteousness. [6]David says the same thing when he speaks of the blessedness of the man to whom God credits righteousness apart from works:

[7]"Blessed are they
  whose transgressions are forgiven,
  whose sins are covered.
[8]Blessed is the man
  whose sin the Lord will never count against him."

> 1. *What is the difference between works and credit? How was Abraham credited with righteousness? Did he earn it? Do we? So how do we get it?*

*2. What does it mean that Abraham did not work for his righteous-
ness? Didn't Abraham obey God? Did that not earn righteousness?*

*3. According to David, what does not count against us? Does that
mean we can sin with no consequences?*

DAY TWO READING AND QUESTIONS

[9]Is this blessedness only for the circumcised, or also for the uncircumcised? We have been saying that Abraham's faith was credited to
him as righteousness. [10]Under what circumstances was it credited?
Was it after he was circumcised, or before? It was not after, but before!
[11]And he received the sign of circumcision, a seal of the righteousness
that he had by faith while he was still uncircumcised. So then, he is
the father of all who believe but have not been circumcised, in order
that righteousness might be credited to them. [12]And he is also the
father of the circumcised who not only are circumcised but who also
walk in the footsteps of the faith that our father Abraham had before
he was circumcised.

[13]It was not through law that Abraham and his offspring received
the promise that he would be heir of the world, but through the righteousness that comes by faith. [14]For if those who live by law are heirs,
faith has no value and the promise is worthless, [15]because law brings
wrath. And where there is no law there is no transgression.

*1. What is the significance of Abraham being righteous by faith before
he was circumcised?*

2. What does "law" do and not do in this passage?

3. If the law is so harmful, why does God give us law?

Day Three Reading and Questions

[16]Therefore, the promise comes by faith, so that it may be by grace and may be guaranteed to all Abraham's offspring-not only to those who are of the law but also to those who are of the faith of Abraham. He is the father of us all. [17]As it is written: "I have made you a father of many nations." He is our father in the sight of God, in whom he believed—the God who gives life to the dead and calls things that are not as though they were.

1. *How is Abraham the father of us all? How should we be like Abraham our father?*

2. *What is the relation between faith and grace?*

3. *What does it mean that "God calls things that are not as if they are"?*

Day Four Reading and Questions

[18]Against all hope, Abraham in hope believed and so became the father of many nations, just as it had been said to him, "So shall your offspring be." [19]Without weakening in his faith, he faced the fact that his body was as good as dead—since he was about a hundred years old-and that Sarah's womb was also dead. [20]Yet he did not waver through unbelief regarding the promise of God, but was strengthened in his faith and gave glory to God, [21]being fully persuaded that God had power to do what he had promised. [22]This is why "it was credited to him as righteousness." [23]The words "it was credited to him" were written not for him alone, [24]but also for us, to whom God will credit righteousness—for us who believe in him who raised Jesus our Lord

from the dead. [25]He was delivered over to death for our sins and was raised to life for our justification.

1. *What is the relationship between faith and hope in Abraham's life? In our lives?*

2. *What promise was so hard for Abraham to believe? Would you have found the promise to Abraham hard to believe?*

3. *What promise of God are we asked to believe in this passage? Do you find that hard?*

Day Five Reading and Questions

Go back and read the entire passage.

1. *Contrast faith and works in this passage. How do they play out in the life of Abraham? In our life in Christ?*

2. *Look at the way "promise" is used in this chapter. How does promise relate to faith? To law? To hope?*

3. *What has God promised us?*

MEDITATION ON ROMANS 4:1-25

"That one doesn't count." Do you remember saying those words as a kid, playing in the neighborhood? After a bad throw or kick, all you had to say was, "That one doesn't count," and you got to try again. In a friendly game of golf, it's called "taking a mulligan."

If only one could do that in the rest of life. After saying harsh words, making a terrible decision, or being caught in an embarrassing situation, one could just say, "That one doesn't count" and it would all go away.

But with God, that's exactly how it is. Our worst, most embarrassing sins do not count. "Blessed is the man whose sin the Lord will never count against him," David says. What a blessing that is! My sins do not count!

Can it be that easy? That simple? Don't we need to wallow in our guilt for a while? Don't we need good deeds to balance out our sins? Don't we need to try harder?

No. It really is that easy. We do not work for our salvation like a wage-earner works for pay. God simply grants us forgiveness. Free. Clear. No strings attached.

So does God not take our sin seriously? After all, "do overs" and mulligans are not allowed in professional sports. You don't even find them in youth leagues. They only happen when those involved do not take the game too seriously. But Paul has just reminded us of the wrath of God, that he does take sin seriously.

So how can sins not count? Because of grace. Because of Jesus. But surely we must do something to get that grace? No, not "do something" in the sense of earning it. All we must do is accept it in faith. All we must do is believe God when he says, "None of you sins count. All are covered by my grace."

But that is hard to believe. As hard as it was for Abraham to believe he and Sarah would have a child. It means hoping when there is no hope. It means trusting when we feel our sins are too great to be forgiven. It means believing, "That one doesn't count."

"Father, increase my faith in your power to do the impossible, to forgive even my deepest, most embarrassing sin. Give me grace to forgive myself and others."

PEACE, JOY, LIFE
(ROMANS 5:1-21)

Day One Reading and Questions

¹Therefore, since we have been justified through faith, we have peace with God through our Lord Jesus Christ, ²through whom we have gained access by faith into this grace in which we now stand. And we rejoice in the hope of the glory of God.

1. *What does it mean to be justified through faith? What do we believe or trust in for our justification?*

2. *What comes to mind when you hear the word, "peace"? What exactly is peace with God?*

3. *What does "hope" mean? What makes us sure of our hope?*

Day Two Reading and Questions

³Not only so, but we also rejoice in our sufferings, because we know that suffering produces perseverance; ⁴perseverance, character; and character, hope. ⁵And hope does not disappoint us, because God has poured out his love into our hearts by the Holy Spirit, whom he has given us.

[6]You see, at just the right time, when we were still powerless, Christ died for the ungodly.

> *1. What is the relationship between peace with God and suffering? How can one have peace in suffering?*

> *2. What does suffering do for us?*

> *3. In what way were we powerless?*

DAY THREE READING AND QUESTIONS

[7]Very rarely will anyone die for a righteous man, though for a good man someone might possibly dare to die. [8]But God demonstrates his own love for us in this: While we were still sinners, Christ died for us.

[9]Since we have now been justified by his blood, how much more shall we be saved from God's wrath through him! [10]For if, when we were God's enemies, we were reconciled to him through the death of his Son, how much more, having been reconciled, shall we be saved through his life! [11]Not only is this so, but we also rejoice in God through our Lord Jesus Christ, through whom we have now received reconciliation.

> *1. How were we enemies of God? How did God treat us when we were enemies?*

> *2. What does it mean to be saved through the life of Jesus? How is this different from being reconciled by his life?*

> *3. What is reconciliation?*

Day Four Reading and Questions

[12]Therefore, just as sin entered the world through one man, and death through sin, and in this way death came to all men, because all sinned— [13]for before the law was given, sin was in the world. But sin is not taken into account when there is no law. [14]Nevertheless, death reigned from the time of Adam to the time of Moses, even over those who did not sin by breaking a command, as did Adam, who was a pattern of the one to come.

[15]But the gift is not like the trespass. For if the many died by the trespass of the one man, how much more did God's grace and the gift that came by the grace of the one man, Jesus Christ, overflow to the many! [16]Again, the gift of God is not like the result of the one man's sin: The judgment followed one sin and brought condemnation, but the gift followed many trespasses and brought justification. [17]For if, by the trespass of the one man, death reigned through that one man, how much more will those who receive God's abundant provision of grace and of the gift of righteousness reign in life through the one man, Jesus Christ.

[18]Consequently, just as the result of one trespass was condemnation for all men, so also the result of one act of righteousness was justification that brings life for all men. [19]For just as through the disobedience of the one man the many were made sinners, so also through the obedience of the one man the many will be made righteous.

[20]The law was added so that the trespass might increase. But where sin increased, grace increased all the more, [21]so that, just as sin reigned in death, so also grace might reign through righteousness to bring eternal life through Jesus Christ our Lord.

> *1. Contrast Adam and Jesus in this passage. How has Jesus undone the harm brought by Adam?*

2. *Why was the law added? Why would God want the trespass to increase? Does God want us to sin?*

3. *Can one "out-sin" the grace of God? Why or why not?*

DAY FIVE READING AND QUESTIONS

Go back and read the entire passage.

1. *What is the relationship between peace with God and reconciliation?*

2. *How should we live as reconciled people? What difference does this make in our relationship with God? With others?*

3. *We have been made righteous by the obedience of Jesus. Do you think of yourself as righteous? Why or why not?*

MEDITATION ON ROMANS 5:1-21.

Peace. Just a rich word. Peace. Such an overused word.

What is peace? The absence of war? Or is it victory in war, when our side can impose "peace" on the other side? What is personal peace with others? Being left alone? Or is it a deep, solid relationship with someone?

What is peace with God? Why should we need peace with God? Paul has already made that clear. We have failed to recognize God. We have failed to obey him. We have sinned and fallen short of what he made us to be.

Some may feel they already have peace with God. "I leave him alone and he leaves me alone," they may say. But peace is not lack of relationship; it is the deepest of relationships. The truth is that God has not and will not leave us alone. He has reconciled us to him through the gift of his Son. He has undone all the damage Adam and his children have done. He has started humanity anew through Jesus.

So we have peace with God, a deep, abiding, loving relationship. But this peace does not mean the absence of trouble. Suffering still comes. Yet even suffering is turned to joy by the hope we have in Christ. Even in suffering, our loving God pours his love into our hearts through the Holy Spirit he has given us.

Peace. Joy. Hope. Life. Righteousness. Love. All big words, big ideas. But all inadequate to describe the gift, the grace, God gives. He gives himself. He gives his Spirit.

"Father, in a world of trouble, you give us peace. Today, pour your love in us through your Holy Spirit. Give us peace in suffering, hope in despair, grace in sin."

SET FREE!
(ROMANS 6:1-7:6)

Day One Reading and Questions

[1]What shall we say, then? Shall we go on sinning so that grace may increase? [2]By no means! We died to sin; how can we live in it any longer? [3]Or don't you know that all of us who were baptized into Christ Jesus were baptized into his death? [4]We were therefore buried with him through baptism into death in order that, just as Christ was raised from the dead through the glory of the Father, we too may live a new life.

[5]If we have been united with him like this in his death, we will certainly also be united with him in his resurrection. [6]For we know that our old self was crucified with him so that the body of sin might be done away with, that we should no longer be slaves to sin— [7]because anyone who has died has been freed from sin.

1. *Why would anyone think that we should go on sinning? How is this a misunderstanding of grace?*

2. *Why does Paul discuss baptism here? Aren't these people already baptized?*

3. *We died with Christ in baptism. Anyone dead is free from sin. Do you feel free from sin? Why or why not? Should you feel that way?*

DAY TWO READING AND QUESTIONS

[8]Now if we died with Christ, we believe that we will also live with him. [9]For we know that since Christ was raised from the dead, he cannot die again; death no longer has mastery over him. [10]The death he died, he died to sin once for all; but the life he lives, he lives to God.

[11]In the same way, count yourselves dead to sin but alive to God in Christ Jesus. [12]Therefore do not let sin reign in your mortal body so that you obey its evil desires. [13]Do not offer the parts of your body to sin, as instruments of wickedness, but rather offer yourselves to God, as those who have been brought from death to life; and offer the parts of your body to him as instruments of righteousness. [14]For sin shall not be your master, because you are not under law, but under grace.

1. What does it mean to be baptized into Christ? How are we in Christ?

2. What does it mean to count ourselves dead to sin but alive to God?

3. How does being under grace free us from sin mastering us? Do we think grace leads people to sin more or sin less? Don't people need law to keep from sinning?

DAY THREE READING AND QUESTIONS

[15]What then? Shall we sin because we are not under law but under grace? By no means! [16]Don't you know that when you offer yourselves to someone to obey him as slaves, you are slaves to the one whom you obey—whether you are slaves to sin, which leads to death, or to obedience, which leads to righteousness? [17]But thanks be to God that, though you used to be slaves to sin, you wholeheartedly obeyed the

form of teaching to which you were entrusted. [18]You have been set free from sin and have become slaves to righteousness.

[19]I put this in human terms because you are weak in your natural selves. Just as you used to offer the parts of your body in slavery to impurity and to ever-increasing wickedness, so now offer them in slavery to righteousness leading to holiness. [20]When you were slaves to sin, you were free from the control of righteousness. [21]What benefit did you reap at that time from the things you are now ashamed of? Those things result in death! [22]But now that you have been set free from sin and have become slaves to God, the benefit you reap leads to holiness, and the result is eternal life. [23]For the wages of sin is death, but the gift of God is eternal life in Christ Jesus our Lord.

1. *In what ways were we slaves to sin? How are we now slaves to righteousness?*

2. *How are we dead to the law?*

3. *What is eternal life in this passage? Is it more than merely living forever?*

Day Four Reading and Questions

[1]Do you not know, brothers—for I am speaking to men who know the law—that the law has authority over a man only as long as he lives? [2]For example, by law a married woman is bound to her husband as long as he is alive, but if her husband dies, she is released from the law of marriage. [3]So then, if she marries another man while her husband is still alive, she is called an adulteress. But if her husband dies, she is released from that law and is not an adulteress, even though she marries another man.

[4]So, my brothers, you also died to the law through the body of Christ, that you might belong to another, to him who was raised from the dead, in order that we might bear fruit to God. [5]For when we were controlled by the sinful nature, the sinful passions aroused by the law were at work in our bodies, so that we bore fruit for death. [6]But now, by dying to what once bound us, we have been released from the law so that we serve in the new way of the Spirit, and not in the old way of the written code.

1. What is the point of the marriage illustration here?

2. How are we dead to the law? Is there no law for Christians?

3. What two "ways" are mentioned here? What is the difference between them?

Day Five Reading and Questions

Go back and read the entire passage.

1. How is our baptism an ongoing experience as opposed to merely a one-time "been there, done that" act?

2. What things are we freed from (or dead to) in this passage?

3. What are we free to do in this passage?

MEDITATION ON ROMANS 6:1-7:6

Freedom. Few words are more precious. We treasure our freedom. We associate freedom with choice, with possibilities, with hope.

What are we free from in Christ? We are free from sin. But if that is true, why do so many of us live in fear and guilt? It's because we lack faith in the power of Christ's death. It's because we forget that we died to sin in baptism. Yes, we still sin, but those sins do not count against us. We are free from slavery to sin. We have the choice to consider ourselves free from sin.

We are free from death. What can that mean? Do Christians not die? We know they do. We know we will. What's more, we know we already have died. Death no longer has mastery over us, because we have died with Christ in baptism. The life we live is not our own; it is the life of the resurrected Jesus in us. Even our physical death will not be the end, but a continuation of our new life in Christ.

We are free from law. Surely, that can't be right. Christians enforce rules and laws more than anyone. But we shouldn't. We are free from law. We are under grace.

But freedom is more than being free from restrictions. It is also being free to live a new way. In Christ, we are free to be slaves of right-eousness. We are free to belong to a new husband, not the old dead husband of the law, but to belong to Jesus. We are free not to have our own way, not to serve ourselves, but to serve in the Spirit's new way.

Too many times Christians are not on the side of freedom. Our reputation (at least partially deserved) is that we want stricter laws and rules. But death has set us free from the law, from sin, and from selfish-ness. We died with Christ in baptism. We live a new life in him through resurrection. A life of liberty. Freedom. Choice. Possibilities. Hope.

"Lord Jesus, remind us constantly that we died with you, we live in you, and we live for you. May we live that life in freedom of the Spirit."

NO CONDEMNATION!

(ROMANS 7:7-8:4)

Day One Reading and Questions

[7]What shall we say, then? Is the law sin? Certainly not! Indeed I would not have known what sin was except through the law. For I would not have known what coveting really was if the law had not said, "Do not covet." [8]But sin, seizing the opportunity afforded by the commandment, produced in me every kind of covetous desire. For apart from law, sin is dead. [9]Once I was alive apart from law; but when the commandment came, sin sprang to life and I died. [10]I found that the very commandment that was intended to bring life actually brought death. [11]For sin, seizing the opportunity afforded by the commandment, deceived me, and through the commandment put me to death. [12]So then, the law is holy, and the commandment is holy, righteous and good.

1. *Why might some think the law is sin?*

2. *Is knowing how we sin a good thing?*

3. *If sin is dead apart from law, then isn't the law a bad thing? Why not?*

DAY TWO READING AND QUESTIONS

[13]Did that which is good, then, become death to me? By no means! But in order that sin might be recognized as sin, it produced death in me through what was good, so that through the commandment sin might become utterly sinful.

[14]We know that the law is spiritual; but I am unspiritual, sold as a slave to sin. [15]I do not understand what I do. For what I want to do I do not do, but what I hate I do. [16]And if I do what I do not want to do, I agree that the law is good. [17]As it is, it is no longer I myself who do it, but it is sin living in me. [18]I know that nothing good lives in me, that is, in my sinful nature. For I have the desire to do what is good, but I cannot carry it out. [19]For what I do is not the good I want to do; no, the evil I do not want to do—this I keep on doing. [20]Now if I do what I do not want to do, it is no longer I who do it, but it is sin living in me that does it.

1. *What good is there in sin becoming utterly sinful?*

2. *Does the description Paul gives of himself in this passage sound like most Christians? Like yourself? Would Paul describe himself as unspiritual and wretched?*

3. *What is the "sinful nature" (some translations have "flesh")? Describe it in your own words.*

DAY THREE READING AND QUESTIONS

[21]So I find this law at work: When I want to do good, evil is right there with me. [22]For in my inner being I delight in God's law; [23]but I

see another law at work in the members of my body, waging war against the law of my mind and making me a prisoner of the law of sin at work within my members. [24]What a wretched man I am! Who will rescue me from this body of death? [25]Thanks be to God—through Jesus Christ our Lord!

So then, I myself in my mind am a slave to God's law, but in the sinful nature a slave to the law of sin.

1. *What are the different meanings of the word "law" in 7:13-21. How many laws are described here?*

2. *Earlier Paul said we died to sin. Here he says in his sinful nature he is a slave to the law of sin. Which is true?*

3. *Who rescues us from our inward struggle? How?*

Day Four Reading and Questions

[1]Therefore, there is now no condemnation for those who are in Christ Jesus, [2]because through Christ Jesus the law of the Spirit of life set me free from the law of sin and death. [3]For what the law was powerless to do in that it was weakened by the sinful nature, God did by sending his own Son in the likeness of sinful man to be a sin offering. And so he condemned sin in sinful man, [4]in order that the righteous requirements of the law might be fully met in us, who do not live according to the sinful nature but according to the Spirit.

1. *What two laws are mentioned here? How are they different?*

2. *What was the law powerless to do?*

3. What does it mean that "the righteous requirements of the law might be fully met in us"? Do we perfectly keep the law? How?

Day Five Reading and Questions

Go back and read the entire passage.

1. How do you react to the word "law"? Is it a good word or a bad one? Can law be good? What law?

2. Does "the law of the Spirit of life" mean that one set of laws has been replaced with another for Christians? If not, what does it mean?

3. Do you feel no condemnation as a Christian? Should you?

MEDITATION ON ROMANS 7:7-8:4

Three laws are at work in our lives.

First, there is God's law. For Jews this was the law of Moses. For Gentiles, the law written on their hearts and consciences (Romans 1:18-32). We might think the law of God is harsh. Why does God demand so much? But God's law has always been intended to bless humanity by bringing us into relationship with God. The law is thus holy, righteous, and good (Romans 7:12).

The problem is not with the law of God but with a second law or principle. Paul calls it the law of sin. We want to follow God's law, but find that there is a law or principle inside of us that keeps us from obeying God. We are torn apart, wretched, because we don't always do the good we want and we often do the evil we do not want. Who can deliver us from the inward struggle between the law of God and the law of sin?

God does through Christ. He delivers through a third law, the law of the Spirit of life in Christ. That law sets us free from the law of sin and death (law #2 above). The law of the Spirit, through the sin offering of Christ, fulfils the righteous requirements of God's law (law #1 above).

If all this is true, why do we still feel that inward struggle between God's law and the law of sin? Because we do not trust the power of God through Christ and the Holy Spirit. By faith we are in Christ Jesus. In Christ Jesus there is no condemnation. Let us no longer condemn ourselves for sin. God does not condemn us. Christ does not condemn us. The Spirit does not condemn us. Instead, let us live according to the Spirit. It is his law we follow, the law of no condemnation.

"Father, increase my faith in your grace. Lord Jesus, by your death, take away my condemnation. Holy Spirit, set me free from the law of sin and death."

LIFE IN THE SPIRIT

(ROMANS 8:5-39)

Day One Reading and Questions

[5]Those who live according to the sinful nature have their minds set on what that nature desires; but those who live in accordance with the Spirit have their minds set on what the Spirit desires. [6]The mind of sinful man is death, but the mind controlled by the Spirit is life and peace; [7]the sinful mind is hostile to God. It does not submit to God's law, nor can it do so. [8]Those controlled by the sinful nature cannot please God.

[9]You, however, are controlled not by the sinful nature but by the Spirit, if the Spirit of God lives in you. And if anyone does not have the Spirit of Christ, he does not belong to Christ. [10]But if Christ is in you, your body is dead because of sin, yet your spirit is alive because of righteousness. [11]And if the Spirit of him who raised Jesus from the dead is living in you, he who raised Christ from the dead will also give life to your mortal bodies through his Spirit, who lives in you.

1. How are the two "minds" contrasted here?

2. What does it mean to have the Spirit of Christ?

3. What will God do to our bodies through his Spirit? Is this a present reality or a future one?

Day Two Reading and Questions

[12]Therefore, brothers, we have an obligation—but it is not to the sinful nature, to live according to it. [13]For if you live according to the sinful nature, you will die; but if by the Spirit you put to death the misdeeds of the body, you will live, [14]because those who are led by the Spirit of God are sons of God. [15]For you did not receive a spirit that makes you a slave again to fear, but you received the Spirit of sonship. And by him we cry, "Abba, Father." [16]The Spirit himself testifies with our spirit that we are God's children. [17]Now if we are children, then we are heirs—heirs of God and co-heirs with Christ, if indeed we share in his sufferings in order that we may also share in his glory.

1. Are our bodies good or bad? Did God make them good or bad?

2. What does a spirit of slavery feel like? What does the Spirit of sonship look like?

3. If we are God's children, why do we have to share in Christ's suffering? Does God want his children to suffer? Did he want Christ to suffer?

Day Three Reading and Questions

[18]I consider that our present sufferings are not worth comparing with the glory that will be revealed in us. [19]The creation waits in eager expectation for the sons of God to be revealed. [20]For the creation was subjected to frustration, not by its own choice, but by the will of the one who subjected it, in hope [21]that the creation itself will be liberated from its bondage to decay and brought into the glorious freedom of the children of God.

[22]We know that the whole creation has been groaning as in the pains of childbirth right up to the present time. [23]Not only so, but we ourselves, who have the firstfruits of the Spirit, groan inwardly as we wait eagerly for our adoption as sons, the redemption of our bodies. [24]For in this hope we were saved. But hope that is seen is no hope at all. Who hopes for what he already has? [25]But if we hope for what we do not yet have, we wait for it patiently.

[26]In the same way, the Spirit helps us in our weakness. We do not know what we ought to pray for, but the Spirit himself intercedes for us with groans that words cannot express. [27]And he who searches our hearts knows the mind of the Spirit, because the Spirit intercedes for the saints in accordance with God's will.

1. What is "glory"? Who will share in the glory of God's children?

2. If we are already God's children, in what sense do we eagerly await our adoption?

3. How does the Spirit help us in prayer? Give an example of when you did not know what to pray for.

Day Four Reading and Questions

[28]And we know that in all things God works for the good of those who love him, who have been called according to his purpose. [29]For those God foreknew he also predestined to be conformed to the likeness of his Son, that he might be the firstborn among many brothers. [30]And those he predestined, he also called; those he called, he also justified; those he justified, he also glorified.

[31]What, then, shall we say in response to this? If God is for us, who can be against us? [32]He who did not spare his own Son, but gave

him up for us all—how will he not also, along with him, graciously give us all things? [33]Who will bring any charge against those whom God has chosen? It is God who justifies. [34]Who is he that condemns? Christ Jesus, who died—more than that, who was raised to life—is at the right hand of God and is also interceding for us. [35]Who shall separate us from the love of Christ? Shall trouble or hardship or persecution or famine or nakedness or danger or sword? [36]As it is written:

"For your sake we face death all day long;

we are considered as sheep to be slaughtered."

[37]No, in all these things we are more than conquerors through him who loved us. [38]For I am convinced that neither death nor life, neither angels nor demons, neither the present nor the future, nor any powers, [39]neither height nor depth, nor anything else in all creation, will be able to separate us from the love of God that is in Christ Jesus our Lord.

1. *What does it mean that God works for our good in all things? Is everything that happens God's will? What about bad things?*

2. *What five things does this passage say God has done for us? Briefly define those words.*

3. *Besides the list found here, list some other things that cannot separate us from the love of God.*

Day Five Reading and Questions

Go back and read the entire passage.

1. *Who can condemn those whom God has chosen? Should we condemn ourselves? Why or why not?*

2. What can separate us from the love of God? Do we fear anything on the list Paul gives? Should we?

3. Can we separate ourselves from God's love?

MEDITATION ON ROMANS 8:5-39

Life in the Spirit. What does it look like?

It is a mysterious life. There is something spooky about the Holy Spirit. Not spooky because of that old translation, "Holy Ghost," but mysterious, supernatural, not of this world. The Holy Spirit is the presence of God himself in us. Therefore, life in the Spirit is not ordinary, natural living on our own power. It is a different level, a new form of living.

It boils down to the question, "Who controls your life?" The answer most might give is, "I control my own life." But do we? Don't we all know what it's like to be controlled by others—parents, children, husbands, wives, bosses, schedules. Some of us know what it's like to be controlled by alcohol, drugs, sex, ambition, and a host of other desires. Before the Spirit came to us, we lived according to that selfish, sinful nature—controlled by our own desires.

Now in Christ we are controlled by the Spirit. What does that look like? It is life and resurrection. It looks like family. Through the Spirit we call God, "Abba, Father," the same word Jesus himself used for God. The Spirit assures us that in spite of our failings we are beloved children of God. Living in the Spirit looks like hope even in the face of suffering. Life in the Spirit means we are never on our own. The Spirit is there in us, helping us, speaking our pain to God. He works all things for our good.

Life in the Spirit means nothing can separate us from the love of

God. We are never left on our own to face the challenges of life. This is no longer our life alone. God himself lives in us, forever.

"Spirit of the living God, Spirit of the risen Christ, live in us today. Make us holy. Overcome our suffering. Help us in trouble. Assure us that we are God's children."

GOD, ISRAEL, AND US

(ROMANS 9:1-10:15)

Day One Reading and Questions

[1]I speak the truth in Christ—I am not lying, my conscience confirms it in the Holy Spirit— [2]I have great sorrow and unceasing anguish in my heart. [3]For I could wish that I myself were cursed and cut off from Christ for the sake of my brothers, those of my own race, [4]the people of Israel. Theirs is the adoption as sons; theirs the divine glory, the covenants, the receiving of the law, the temple worship and the promises. [5]Theirs are the patriarchs, and from them is traced the human ancestry of Christ, who is God over all, forever praised! Amen.

[6]It is not as though God's word had failed. For not all who are descended from Israel are Israel. [7]Nor because they are his descendants are they all Abraham's children. On the contrary, "It is through Isaac that your offspring will be reckoned." [8]In other words, it is not the natural children who are God's children, but it is the children of the promise who are regarded as Abraham's offspring. [9]For this was how the promise was stated: "At the appointed time I will return, and Sarah will have a son."

[10]Not only that, but Rebekah's children had one and the same father, our father Isaac. [11]Yet, before the twins were born or had done anything good or bad—in order that God's purpose in election might stand: [12]not by works but by him who calls—she was told, "The older will serve the younger." [13]Just as it is written: "Jacob I loved, but Esau I hated."

1. Does Paul really wish he could be condemned for Israel's sake? Or is he using hyperbole and exaggeration? Why does he feel so strongly about this?

2. List all the blessings that the people of Israel have from God.

3. Is God to blame for Israel's unbelief? What is the point of the Isaac, Jacob, and Esau examples?

Day Two Reading and Questions

[14]What then shall we say? Is God unjust? Not at all! [15]For he says to Moses,

"I will have mercy on whom I have mercy,
and I will have compassion on whom I have compassion."
[16]It does not, therefore, depend on man's desire or effort, but on God's mercy. [17]For the Scripture says to Pharaoh: "I raised you up for this very purpose, that I might display my power in you and that my name might be proclaimed in all the earth." [18]Therefore God has mercy on whom he wants to have mercy, and he hardens whom he wants to harden.

[19]One of you will say to me: "Then why does God still blame us? For who resists his will?" [20]But who are you, O man, to talk back to God? "Shall what is formed say to him who formed it, 'Why did you make me like this?'" [21]Does not the potter have the right to make out of the same lump of clay some pottery for noble purposes and some for common use?

[22]What if God, choosing to show his wrath and make his power known, bore with great patience the objects of his wrath-prepared for destruction? [23]What if he did this to make the riches of his glory known to the objects of his mercy, whom he prepared in advance for glory— [24]even us, whom he also called, not only from the Jews but

also from the Gentiles? [25]As he says in Hosea:

"I will call them 'my people' who are not my people;
    and I will call her 'my loved one' who is not my loved one," [26]and,

"It will happen that in the very place where it was said to them,
    'You are not my people,'
they will be called 'sons of the living God.'"

[27]Isaiah cries out concerning Israel:

"Though the number of the Israelites be like the sand by the sea,
    only the remnant will be saved.
[28]For the Lord will carry out
    his sentence on earth with speed and finality."

[29]It is just as Isaiah said previously:

"Unless the Lord Almighty
    had left us descendants,
we would have become like Sodom,
    we would have been like Gomorrah."

1. Is God fair when he has mercy on some and hardens others?

2. Why can't we accuse God of being unfair?

3. What Old Testament phrases does Paul use to speak of the salvation of Gentiles?

DAY THREE READING AND QUESTIONS

[30]What then shall we say? That the Gentiles, who did not pursue righteousness, have obtained it, a righteousness that is by faith; [31]but Israel, who pursued a law of righteousness, has not attained it. [32]Why not? Because they pursued it not by faith but as if it were by works. They stumbled over the "stumbling stone." [33]As it is written:

"See, I lay in Zion a stone that causes men to stumble
and a rock that makes them fall,
and the one who trusts in him will never be put to shame."

[1]Brothers, my heart's desire and prayer to God for the Israelites is that they may be saved. [2]For I can testify about them that they are zealous for God, but their zeal is not based on knowledge. [3]Since they did not know the righteousness that comes from God and sought to establish their own, they did not submit to God's righteousness. [4]Christ is the end of the law so that there may be righteousness for everyone who believes.

[5]Moses describes in this way the righteousness that is by the law: "The man who does these things will live by them." [6]But the righteousness that is by faith says: "Do not say in your heart, 'Who will ascend into heaven?' (that is, to bring Christ down) [7]or 'Who will descend into the deep?'" (that is, to bring Christ up from the dead). [8]But what does it say? "The word is near you; it is in your mouth and in your heart," that is, the word of faith we are proclaiming: [9]That if you confess with your mouth, "Jesus is Lord," and believe in your heart that God raised him from the dead, you will be saved.

1. Why did the Gentiles obtain righteousness? Why did Israel not obtain it?

2. In what way was Israel's zeal not based on knowledge?

3. Where is the word of God? What does that mean?

Day Four Reading and Questions

[10]For it is with your heart that you believe and are justified, and it is with your mouth that you confess and are saved. [11]As the Scripture

says, "Anyone who trusts in him will never be put to shame." [12]For there is no difference between Jew and Gentile—the same Lord is Lord of all and richly blesses all who call on him, [13]for, "Everyone who calls on the name of the Lord will be saved."

[14]How, then, can they call on the one they have not believed in? And how can they believe in the one of whom they have not heard? And how can they hear without someone preaching to them? [15]And how can they preach unless they are sent? As it is written, "How beautiful are the feet of those who bring good news!"

1. *What must one do to be saved, according to this passage?*

2. *What does the heart do in this passage?*

3. *What is the role of the preacher in this passage?*

DAY FIVE READING AND QUESTIONS

Go back and read the entire passage.

1. *What relevance does this talk of "Israel" have for us today? What lessons can we learn from them?*

2. *Do you find the picture of God in this passage frightening or comforting? Why?*

3. *What does it mean to call upon the Lord? How do we call on him today?*

MEDITATION ON ROMANS 9:1-10:15

Is God unjust? "Nothing can separate us from the love of God." But what happens when those you love the most refuse to accept the grace of God? What about those who have often heard the story of his love, but will not trust that story?

That's the heartbreak Paul faced with his people Israel. They had received the law, the true worship, and the message of the prophets. Yet most of them failed to recognize Jesus as the Messiah. How could that be?

What about our friends and family who will not recognize Jesus? How can anyone fail to accept the free gift of God's love? But they do. Is God to blame? What more can God do? He has given his law, given his Son, sent messengers to them with good news. It's not as though God's word has failed. Some have come to believe. Why not all? Why not those we love so dearly?

Because they will not. What can God do when they refuse his love? He can hurt for them. He can use their refusal to bring others to him. He offers his love to anyone who calls on him.

What can we do about those we love who refuse to trust Jesus? We can tell them the story of Jesus. We can pray they will open their hearts. We can show God's love to them in ways small and great. We can remind them that God's word in the flesh, Jesus Christ, is near them. We might even wish we could be condemned if they only would believe. But we cannot make them believe.

"Father, please move the hearts of those we love so they may trust in your Son Jesus. May we trust your love for them and for us."

KINDNESS AND STERNNESS

(ROMANS 10:16-11:36)

Day One Reading and Questions

[16]But not all the Israelites accepted the good news. For Isaiah says, "Lord, who has believed our message?" [17]Consequently, faith comes from hearing the message, and the message is heard through the word of Christ. [18]But I ask: Did they not hear? Of course they did:

"Their voice has gone out into all the earth,
their words to the ends of the world."

[19]Again I ask: Did Israel not understand? First, Moses says,

"I will make you envious by those who are not a nation;
I will make you angry by a nation that has no understanding."

[20]And Isaiah boldly says,

"I was found by those who did not seek me;
I revealed myself to those who did not ask for me."

[21]But concerning Israel he says,

"All day long I have held out my hands
to a disobedient and obstinate people."

[1]I ask then: Did God reject his people? By no means! I am an Israelite myself, a descendant of Abraham, from the tribe of Benjamin. [2]God did not reject his people, whom he foreknew. Don't you know what the Scripture says in the passage about Elijah—how he appealed to God against Israel: [3]"Lord, they have killed your prophets and torn down your altars; I am the only one left, and they are trying

to kill me." [4]And what was God's answer to him? "I have reserved for myself seven thousand who have not bowed the knee to Baal." [5]So too, at the present time there is a remnant chosen by grace. [6]And if by grace, then it is no longer by works; if it were, grace would no longer be grace.

[7]What then? What Israel sought so earnestly it did not obtain, but the elect did. The others were hardened, [8]as it is written:

"God gave them a spirit of stupor,
    eyes so that they could not see
    and ears so that they could not hear,
    to this very day."

[9]And David says:

"May their table become a snare and a trap,
    a stumbling block and a retribution for them.
[10]May their eyes be darkened so they cannot see,
    and their backs be bent forever."

1. Did Israel hear God's message? Did they understand?

2. What evidence does Paul give that God has not rejected his people Israel?

3. Who in Israel did obtain salvation? How are they described?

DAY TWO READING AND QUESTIONS

[11]Again I ask: Did they stumble so as to fall beyond recovery? Not at all! Rather, because of their transgression, salvation has come to the Gentiles to make Israel envious. [12]But if their transgression means riches for the world, and their loss means riches for the Gentiles, how much greater riches will their fullness bring!

[13]I am talking to you Gentiles. Inasmuch as I am the apostle to the Gentiles, I make much of my ministry [14]in the hope that I may somehow arouse my own people to envy and save some of them. [15]For if their rejection is the reconciliation of the world, what will their acceptance be but life from the dead? [16]If the part of the dough offered as firstfruits is holy, then the whole batch is holy; if the root is holy, so are the branches.

[17]If some of the branches have been broken off, and you, though a wild olive shoot, have been grafted in among the others and now share in the nourishing sap from the olive root, [18]do not boast over those branches. If you do, consider this: You do not support the root, but the root supports you. [19]You will say then, "Branches were broken off so that I could be grafted in." [20]Granted. But they were broken off because of unbelief, and you stand by faith. Do not be arrogant, but be afraid. [21]For if God did not spare the natural branches, he will not spare you either.

1. What is the relationship between Gentiles and Israel in this passage?

2. Explain the olive tree illustration.

3. If Paul is the apostle to the Gentiles, then what is his ministry to the Jews?

Day Three Reading and Questions

[22]Consider therefore the kindness and sternness of God: sternness to those who fell, but kindness to you, provided that you continue in his kindness. Otherwise, you also will be cut off. [23]And if they do not persist in unbelief, they will be grafted in, for God is able to graft them

in again. [24]After all, if you were cut out of an olive tree that is wild by nature, and contrary to nature were grafted into a cultivated olive tree, how much more readily will these, the natural branches, be grafted into their own olive tree!

[25]I do not want you to be ignorant of this mystery, brothers, so that you may not be conceited: Israel has experienced a hardening in part until the full number of the Gentiles has come in. [26]And so all Israel will be saved, as it is written:

"The deliverer will come from Zion;
 he will turn godlessness away from Jacob.
[27]And this is my covenant with them
 when I take away their sins."

[28]As far as the gospel is concerned, they are enemies on your account; but as far as election is concerned, they are loved on account of the patriarchs, [29]for God's gifts and his call are irrevocable. [30]Just as you who were at one time disobedient to God have now received mercy as a result of their disobedience, [31]so they too have now become disobedient in order that they too may now receive mercy as a result of God's mercy to you.

1. What is the relationship between God's kindness and sternness?

2. Paul says, "All Israel will be saved." What does this mean? When will it happen?

3. Why is Israel loved?

DAY FOUR READING AND QUESTIONS

[32]For God has bound all men over to disobedience so that he may have mercy on them all.

[33]Oh, the depth of the riches of the wisdom and knowledge of God!
  How unsearchable his judgments,
  and his paths beyond tracing out!
[34]"Who has known the mind of the Lord?
  Or who has been his counselor?"
[35]"Who has ever given to God,
  that God should repay him?"
[36]For from him and through him and to him are all things.
  To him be the glory forever! Amen.

1. Why has God bound everyone over to disobedience? Does this mean disobedience is a good thing?

2. Can we figure out God? Should we try? Can we keep from trying?

3. If all things are from, through, and to God, what does that imply about our place as humans?

Day Five Reading and Questions

Go back and read the entire passage.

1. Is salvation primarily about us or about God?

2. What does it mean that God's call is irrevocable? Is Israel still God's chosen people? How?

3. What is the point of the doxology (song of praise) in Romans 11:33-36? How does it fit with chapters 9-11?

MEDITATION ON ROMANS 10:16-11:36

"I can't believe in a God who would allow that."

Perhaps we've heard people say something like that. When disasters kill millions, when wars destroy the lives of innocent children, when someone we love dearly suffers unimaginable pain, we might even say something like that ourselves.

"I can't believe in that kind of God."

But what kind of God do we want? Do we really want a God of easy answers, a God we can figure out? Do we want a predictable and "tame" God?

Even if we do, that's not what we have in the Bible. God's ways are not our ways. He is beyond our comprehension. In the Old Testament, he tests Job and when Job demands an answer, God says, "Where were you when I made the world?"

Why do some we love not accept the gospel? What is God's dealing with his people Israel? Why does God allow suffering?

We just don't know. We cannot second-guess his judgment. We cannot follow the ways of the divine mind.

We do not know, but we can trust. Indeed, faith is tested at the point where we cannot fathom God's ways. We might not even like what God is doing, but we trust that he is so big that he can even bring good out of the worst evil. Who knows? It could be that the disobedience of those we love can be used by God to bring others to him.

It's not the way we would do things. But we are not God.

"Lord God, we do not understand your ways, but we praise you as the God who made all things and to whom all things belong. May we praise you in faith this day."

TRANSFORMED LIVES
(ROMANS 12:1-13:7)

Day One Reading and Questions

¹Therefore, I urge you, brothers, in view of God's mercy, to offer your bodies as living sacrifices, holy and pleasing to God—this is your spiritual act of worship. ²Do not conform any longer to the pattern of this world, but be transformed by the renewing of your mind. Then you will be able to test and approve what God's will is—his good, pleasing and perfect will.

1. What does it mean to be a living sacrifice? What does it look like?

2. How is "worship" used in this passage? Is this our usual view of worship? Should all of life be worship or only certain times?

3. What keeps us from becoming conformed to the world?

Day Two Reading and Questions

³For by the grace given me I say to every one of you: Do not think of yourself more highly than you ought, but rather think of yourself with sober judgment, in accordance with the measure of faith God has given you. ⁴Just as each of us has one body with many members,

and these members do not all have the same function, [5]so in Christ we who are many form one body, and each member belongs to all the others. [6]We have different gifts, according to the grace given us. If a man's gift is prophesying, let him use it in proportion to his faith. [7]If it is serving, let him serve; if it is teaching, let him teach; [8]if it is encouraging, let him encourage; if it is contributing to the needs of others, let him give generously; if it is leadership, let him govern diligently; if it is showing mercy, let him do it cheerfully.

1. *If we are not to think more highly of ourselves than we ought, does that mean we should think poorly of ourselves? How should we think?*

2. *What is the point of Paul's body metaphor?*

3. *What gifts are listed here? Are these all the gifts in the body? What gift has God given you?*

Day Three Reading and Questions

[9]Love must be sincere. Hate what is evil; cling to what is good. [10]Be devoted to one another in brotherly love. Honor one another above yourselves. [11]Never be lacking in zeal, but keep your spiritual fervor, serving the Lord. [12]Be joyful in hope, patient in affliction, faithful in prayer. [13]Share with God's people who are in need. Practice hospitality.

[14]Bless those who persecute you; bless and do not curse. [15]Rejoice with those who rejoice; mourn with those who mourn. [16]Live in harmony with one another. Do not be proud, but be willing to associate with people of low position. Do not be conceited.

1. *How is love described in this passage?*

2. What is hospitality? How does one practice it?

3. What sin is condemned most strongly in this passage? What virtue is promoted the most? What does this say about being a living sacrifice?

DAY FOUR READING AND QUESTIONS

[17]Do not repay anyone evil for evil. Be careful to do what is right in the eyes of everybody. [18]If it is possible, as far as it depends on you, live at peace with everyone. [19]Do not take revenge, my friends, but leave room for God's wrath, for it is written: "It is mine to avenge; I will repay," says the Lord. [20]On the contrary:

"If your enemy is hungry, feed him;

if he is thirsty, give him something to drink.

In doing this, you will heap burning coals on his head."

[21]Do not be overcome by evil, but overcome evil with good.

[1]Everyone must submit himself to the governing authorities, for there is no authority except that which God has established. The authorities that exist have been established by God. [2]Consequently, he who rebels against the authority is rebelling against what God has instituted, and those who do so will bring judgment on themselves. [3]For rulers hold no terror for those who do right, but for those who do wrong. Do you want to be free from fear of the one in authority? Then do what is right and he will commend you. [4]For he is God's servant to do you good. But if you do wrong, be afraid, for he does not bear the sword for nothing. He is God's servant, an agent of wrath to bring punishment on the wrongdoer. [5]Therefore, it is necessary to submit to the authorities, not only because of possible punishment but also because of conscience.

[6]This is also why you pay taxes, for the authorities are God's

servants, who give their full time to governing. ⁷Give everyone what you owe him: If you owe taxes, pay taxes; if revenue, then revenue; if respect, then respect; if honor, then honor.

> 1. *Should Christians ever take revenge on someone who has wronged them? Should we want God to avenge us? Why or why not?*

> 2. *What is the relationship between the prohibition of vengeance and the section on government? What is the role of government according to Paul?*

> 3. *Does God approve of all governments? Does he approve all that even "good" governments do?*

DAY FIVE READING AND QUESTIONS

Go back and read the entire passage.

> 1. *Offering our bodies as sacrifices may sound individualistic. According to this passage, how does this offering affect how we treat others?*

> 2. *Are you usually tempted to think more highly of yourself? Do you think the gifts God has given you are better than those he gives others? Are they worse?*

> 3. *Is love for enemies optional? Is it at the heart of being a living sacrifice? List some specific ways we can show love for our enemies.*

MEDITATION ON ROMANS 12:1-13:7

How do we respond to the incredible mercy of God? Through Christ, he has forgiven every sin. Sins no longer count against us. He has given us peace, hope, love. He has redeemed us from an empty life. He has brought us back to him. He has given us his Holy Spirit, and nothing in all creation can separate us from his love.

All free. All by grace. It all costs us nothing.

We cannot repay his love. We need not. It is free. But such matchless love calls for a response.

We give him all that we are. Our bodies. Living sacrifices, so that everything we do in the body we do for him. We give our bodies for his body—the church. We don't think too highly of ourselves, but use the gifts he has given us for others. We give him love.

We give that love to him by giving it to others, even those who are our enemies. God punishes evil through governments and he will punish evil in the last day. But it is God who avenges, not we. In light of his great mercy, we feed our enemies, overcoming evil with good.

In view of God's mercy, the only response is to love him with all that we are. That may sound easy. What is hard is loving those who hurt us. Turning the other cheek. Going the extra mile. Returning good for evil. But that is the living sacrifice we are called to make. Jesus made the same sacrifice for us.

"Father, turn our hearts to you. Remind us of your great love for us even when we were enemies, so we in turn can love our enemies with your mercy."

STOP JUDGING

(ROMANS 13:8-15:7)

Day One Reading and Questions

⁸Let no debt remain outstanding, except the continuing debt to love one another, for he who loves his fellowman has fulfilled the law. ⁹The commandments, "Do not commit adultery," "Do not murder," "Do not steal," "Do not covet," and whatever other commandment there may be, are summed up in this one rule: "Love your neighbor as yourself." ¹⁰Love does no harm to its neighbor. Therefore love is the fulfillment of the law.

¹¹And do this, understanding the present time. The hour has come for you to wake up from your slumber, because our salvation is nearer now than when we first believed. ¹²The night is nearly over; the day is almost here. So let us put aside the deeds of darkness and put on the armor of light. ¹³Let us behave decently, as in the daytime, not in orgies and drunkenness, not in sexual immorality and debauchery, not in dissension and jealousy. ¹⁴Rather, clothe yourselves with the Lord Jesus Christ, and do not think about how to gratify the desires of the sinful nature.

1. What is the greatest debt we owe?

2. What does it mean that our salvation is nearer now?

3. How should we wait for the coming of Jesus?

Day Two Reading and Questions

[1]Accept him whose faith is weak, without passing judgment on disputable matters. [2]One man's faith allows him to eat everything, but another man, whose faith is weak, eats only vegetables. [3]The man who eats everything must not look down on him who does not, and the man who does not eat everything must not condemn the man who does, for God has accepted him. [4]Who are you to judge someone else's servant? To his own master he stands or falls. And he will stand, for the Lord is able to make him stand.

> *1. What does it mean to be "weak" in this passage? Is the weak one here less Christian than the strong one?*

> *2. How should the strong treat the weak? How should the weak treat the strong?*

> *3. Who judges us? How does he judge?*

Day Three Reading and Questions

[5]One man considers one day more sacred than another; another man considers every day alike. Each one should be fully convinced in his own mind. [6]He who regards one day as special, does so to the Lord. He who eats meat, eats to the Lord, for he gives thanks to God; and he who abstains, does so to the Lord and gives thanks to God. [7]For none of us lives to himself alone and none of us dies to himself alone. [8]If we live, we live to the Lord; and if we die, we die to the Lord. So, whether we live or die, we belong to the Lord.

[9]For this very reason, Christ died and returned to life so that he

might be the Lord of both the dead and the living. [10]You, then, why do you judge your brother? Or why do you look down on your brother? For we will all stand before God's judgment seat. [11]It is written:

"'As surely as I live,' says the Lord,
  'every knee will bow before me;
  every tongue will confess to God.'"

[12]So then, each of us will give an account of himself to God.

1. *Can two Christians each be fully convinced of opposite beliefs? Which one is right? What makes them right?*

2. *What is more important than being "right" on religious issues?*

3. *Who will we have to account for before God? What does that imply about judging others?*

Day Four Reading and Questions

[13]Therefore let us stop passing judgment on one another. Instead, make up your mind not to put any stumbling block or obstacle in your brother's way. [14]As one who is in the Lord Jesus, I am fully convinced that no food is unclean in itself. But if anyone regards something as unclean, then for him it is unclean. [15]If your brother is distressed because of what you eat, you are no longer acting in love. Do not by your eating destroy your brother for whom Christ died. [16]Do not allow what you consider good to be spoken of as evil. [17]For the kingdom of God is not a matter of eating and drinking, but of righteousness, peace and joy in the Holy Spirit, [18]because anyone who serves Christ in this way is pleasing to God and approved by men.

[19]Let us therefore make every effort to do what leads to peace and to mutual edification. [20]Do not destroy the work of God for the sake of

food. All food is clean, but it is wrong for a man to eat anything that causes someone else to stumble. [21]It is better not to eat meat or drink wine or to do anything else that will cause your brother to fall.

[22]So whatever you believe about these things keep between yourself and God. Blessed is the man who does not condemn himself by what he approves. [23]But the man who has doubts is condemned if he eats, because his eating is not from faith; and everything that does not come from faith is sin.

[1]We who are strong ought to bear with the failings of the weak and not to please ourselves. [2]Each of us should please his neighbor for his good, to build him up. [3]For even Christ did not please himself but, as it is written: "The insults of those who insult you have fallen on me." [4]For everything that was written in the past was written to teach us, so that through endurance and the encouragement of the Scriptures we might have hope.

[5]May the God who gives endurance and encouragement give you a spirit of unity among yourselves as you follow Christ Jesus, [6]so that with one heart and mouth you may glorify the God and Father of our Lord Jesus Christ.

[7]Accept one another, then, just as Christ accepted you, in order to bring praise to God.

1. *How do we put stumbling blocks or obstacles before our brothers and sisters?*

2. *How can insisting on our rights (or on our "being right") destroy our brothers and sisters?*

3. *What does it mean to cause a brother or sister to stumble? Is this more than upsetting them?*

Day Five Reading and Questions

Go back and read the entire passage.

1. *List some ways Christ did not please himself. What "rights" did Christ give up to save us?*

2. *What does the "spirit of unity" look like in this passage? Does unity mean agreement?*

3. *Why is it so hard for us to "accept one another" as we are?*

MEDITATION ON ROMANS 13:8-15:7

Love. Everyone is for love.

"Love your neighbor as yourself." No one objects to loving the neighbor.

But what if your neighbor is wrong? What if this "neighbor" is a fellow Christian who disagrees strongly with you? How can we love our brothers and sisters who misunderstand the Bible? After studying with them, do we write them off as false Christians who will not accept the obvious truth? Or do we love them as full brothers and sisters in spite of their "error"?

Paul clearly says we should love and accept them. He says, "Do not judge your brother or sister." He commands, "Do not look down on your brother or sister." The specific issues of disagreement he mentions—eating meat, keeping holy days, and drinking wine—may not seem that important to us. But they were important to some Roman Christians. Those Christians lined up strongly on opposite sides of theses issues, each side firmly convinced that the other was wrong. Each thought the Bible was on their side. Paul doesn't resolve the issues, but he pleads for love in spite of their differences.

We can think of other issues that divide Christians, some we think are important, even central to the faith. But it is not agreement that unites us; it is the love of God in Christ. Even if our brothers and sisters are wrong, we leave their judgment to Christ. Even if we are wrong (and we have been before), we leave our judgment in the hands of a gracious Savior.

Love is not real until the fire of disagreement tests it. Love for our neighbor is difficult. It also is urgent. Our salvation is nearer now than when we first believed. The one who is Love himself will return and take us to be with him forever. As we wait, it is time to put aside dark deeds, whether the selfishness of sexual immorality or self-centered dissention and jealousy. We must become like the One for whom we wait. Jesus comes as one who did not please himself. We dare not try to wait for him by insisting that others please us. Love for our brothers and sisters, especially when they are wrong, is the love of God that gives us a spirit of unity so we can glorify God with one heart and one voice.

"God of love, give us the gift of love and unity. Lord Jesus, live in us so that we may please others, not ourselves. Holy Spirit, make us one in spite of our differences."

MISSIONARIES

(ROMANS 15:8-16:27)

DAY ONE READING AND QUESTIONS

[8]For I tell you that Christ has become a servant of the Jews on behalf of God's truth, to confirm the promises made to the patriarchs [9]so that the Gentiles may glorify God for his mercy, as it is written:

"Therefore I will praise you among the Gentiles;
  I will sing hymns to your name."

[10]Again, it says,

"Rejoice, O Gentiles, with his people."

[11]And again,

"Praise the Lord, all you Gentiles,
  and sing praises to him, all you peoples."

[12]And again, Isaiah says,

"The Root of Jesse will spring up,
  one who will arise to rule over the nations;
  the Gentiles will hope in him."

[13]May the God of hope fill you with all joy and peace as you trust in him, so that you may overflow with hope by the power of the Holy Spirit.

[14]I myself am convinced, my brothers, that you yourselves are full of goodness, complete in knowledge and competent to instruct one another. [15]I have written you quite boldly on some points, as if to remind you of them again, because of the grace God gave me [16]to be a

minister of Christ Jesus to the Gentiles with the priestly duty of proclaiming the gospel of God, so that the Gentiles might become an offering acceptable to God, sanctified by the Holy Spirit.

[17]Therefore I glory in Christ Jesus in my service to God. [18]I will not venture to speak of anything except what Christ has accomplished through me in leading the Gentiles to obey God by what I have said and done— [19]by the power of signs and miracles, through the power of the Spirit. So from Jerusalem all the way around to Illyricum, I have fully proclaimed the gospel of Christ. [20]It has always been my ambition to preach the gospel where Christ was not known, so that I would not be building on someone else's foundation. [21]Rather, as it is written:

"Those who were not told about him will see,

and those who have not heard will understand."

[22]This is why I have often been hindered from coming to you.

1. *What is the point of the Old Testament quotations in Romans 15:9-12? Do these verses speak to you? How?*

2. *How does Paul describe his mission to the Gentiles? What was his duty?*

3. *Where did Paul choose to preach? Why?*

Day Two Reading and Questions

[23]But now that there is no more place for me to work in these regions, and since I have been longing for many years to see you, [24]I plan to do so when I go to Spain. I hope to visit you while passing through and to have you assist me on my journey there, after I have enjoyed your company for a while. [25]Now, however, I am on my way to Jerusalem in the service of the saints there. [26]For Macedonia and

Achaia were pleased to make a contribution for the poor among the saints in Jerusalem. [27]They were pleased to do it, and indeed they owe it to them. For if the Gentiles have shared in the Jews' spiritual blessings, they owe it to the Jews to share with them their material blessings. [28]So after I have completed this task and have made sure that they have received this fruit, I will go to Spain and visit you on the way. [29]I know that when I come to you, I will come in the full measure of the blessing of Christ.

[30]I urge you, brothers, by our Lord Jesus Christ and by the love of the Spirit, to join me in my struggle by praying to God for me. [31]Pray that I may be rescued from the unbelievers in Judea and that my service in Jerusalem may be acceptable to the saints there, [32]so that by God's will I may come to you with joy and together with you be refreshed. [33]The God of peace be with you all. Amen.

1. *Where is Paul going when he writes this letter? Why? Where does he plan to go after that?*

2. *What is the relationship between spiritual blessings and material blessings?*

3. *What does Paul want the Romans to pray concerning him?*

DAY THREE READING AND QUESTIONS

[1]I commend to you our sister Phoebe, a servant of the church in Cenchrea. [2]I ask you to receive her in the Lord in a way worthy of the saints and to give her any help she may need from you, for she has been a great help to many people, including me.

[3]Greet Priscilla and Aquila, my fellow workers in Christ Jesus. [4]They risked their lives for me. Not only I but all the churches of the

Gentiles are grateful to them.

⁵Greet also the church that meets at their house.

Greet my dear friend Epenetus, who was the first convert to Christ in the province of Asia.

⁶Greet Mary, who worked very hard for you.

⁷Greet Andronicus and Junias, my relatives who have been in prison with me. They are outstanding among the apostles, and they were in Christ before I was.

⁸Greet Ampliatus, whom I love in the Lord.

⁹Greet Urbanus, our fellow worker in Christ, and my dear friend Stachys.

¹⁰Greet Apelles, tested and approved in Christ.

Greet those who belong to the household of Aristobulus.

¹¹Greet Herodion, my relative.

Greet those in the household of Narcissus who are in the Lord.

¹²Greet Tryphena and Tryphosa, those women who work hard in the Lord.

Greet my dear friend Persis, another woman who has worked very hard in the Lord.

¹³Greet Rufus, chosen in the Lord, and his mother, who has been a mother to me, too.

¹⁴Greet Asyncritus, Phlegon, Hermes, Patrobas, Hermas and the brothers with them.

¹⁵Greet Philologus, Julia, Nereus and his sister, and Olympas and all the saints with them.

¹⁶Greet one another with a holy kiss. All the churches of Christ send greetings.

1. List the women mentioned in this chapter. How are they described? What does this say about their work in the early church?

2. Why do you think Paul greets so many people by name in this

2222222222222222

chapter? How does this relate to his purpose for writing the letter?

3. How do you imagine house churches? How big were they? What was the "feel" of their assembly?

Day Four Reading and Questions

[17]I urge you, brothers, to watch out for those who cause divisions and put obstacles in your way that are contrary to the teaching you have learned. Keep away from them. [18]For such people are not serving our Lord Christ, but their own appetites. By smooth talk and flattery they deceive the minds of naive people. [19]Everyone has heard about your obedience, so I am full of joy over you; but I want you to be wise about what is good, and innocent about what is evil.

[20]The God of peace will soon crush Satan under your feet.

The grace of our Lord Jesus be with you.

[21]Timothy, my fellow worker, sends his greetings to you, as do Lucius, Jason and Sosipater, my relatives.

[22]I, Tertius, who wrote down this letter, greet you in the Lord.

[23]Gaius, whose hospitality I and the whole church here enjoy, sends you his greetings.

[24]Erastus, who is the city's director of public works, and our brother Quartus send you their greetings.

[25]Now to him who is able to establish you by my gospel and the proclamation of Jesus Christ, according to the revelation of the mystery hidden for long ages past, [26]but now revealed and made known through the prophetic writings by the command of the eternal God, so that all nations might believe and obey him— [27]to the only wise God be glory forever through Jesus Christ! Amen.

1. What group are the Romans told to keep way from? Why?

2. Gaius is praised for his hospitality. What is hospitality? How do we practice it today?

3. How does this letter end? Why is that significant?

DAY FIVE READING AND QUESTIONS

Go back and read the entire passage.

1. Paul calls God the God of Jew and Gentile. Is he the God of all today? Hindu? Muslim? Unbelievers? How is he their God? What implications does this have for us as Christians?

2. Paul says he will speak of nothing except what Christ has accomplished through him (Romans 15:18). What has Christ accomplished through you? Have you spoken of it? What is the place of witnessing to others?

3. If you were writing a letter to a church you once belonged to, whom would you greet by name? Why those particular people?

MEDITATION ON ROMANS 15:8-16:27

Paul describes his life work this way: "I will not venture to speak of anything except what Christ has accomplished through me…" (Romans 15:17). And think of all Christ had done through Paul—proclaimed the good news, planted churches, and persisted in spite of persecution.

Wouldn't we all like to be a Paul? Shouldn't we aspire to be like him?

Yes and no. No, we are not all called to be a Paul—an apostle, a missionary, and an evangelist. Yes, like Paul we are called to allow Christ to live in us. Christ speaks and accomplishes great things in us, just as he did in Paul. But he does not call us to be Paul; he calls us to be who we should be in our particular situations.

That's one reason for all the names listed in chapter sixteen. Some of these men and women are called apostles (that is, missionaries), but most are described as hard workers in Christ. We are not all Paul. There was only one. God does not want us to all be like Paul in every way—single, a rabbi, an apostle. What he wants is for us to be who we should be in Christ. He wants us to respond to his grace by working hard in the Lord. In other words, to speak only of what Christ has done for us.

We may not be Paul or Priscilla or even Rufus. I can be the Gary God wants me to be in Christ. By the love and power of the Holy Spirit, we can be Christ where we are. We can avoid division, love our brothers and sisters in Christ, and proclaim in our own unique way what Christ is doing for us.

That is the power of the good news.

"Christ, live in us this day through your Holy Spirit. May we not seek to be famous Christians, but desire to speak only what you have done in us."

THE SPIRITUALITY OF GALATIANS

Galatians is a letter from a missionary who is deeply concerned about a group of churches. Paul's language in this letter is sometimes strong and even harsh. That harshness stems not from his anger with the Galatians, but from his genuine care for them. Paul fears that they have deserted the good news of freedom in Jesus for a false gospel that will be a return to spiritual slavery.

Because Paul's language is at times sharp, we might miss the deep spiritual message of this letter. Paul is not defending himself but the truth of his message. The story of Jesus was not made up by Paul or even passed on to Paul like a worn, second-hand tale. Instead, it came to Paul as a revelation from God. The Galatians (and we) should trust that message not only because it is from God, but because it power-fully changed the life of Paul from persecutor to apostle. That same good news changes us from slaves to free children of God. As God's children, we show his love to others.

The spirituality of Galatians revolves around these three themes: trust, freedom, and love.

TRUSTING THE MESSAGE

Paul goes to great lengths to show the gospel he proclaims is not from human beings but from God (Galatians 1:11-2:10). We must trust that message of good news and not trust our ability to keep

God's law on our own (Galatians 2:15-3:25). Trusting that gospel is a personal trust in the God who keeps his promises. Our very lives are sustained by faith or trust in the Son of God who gave himself for us (Galatians 2:20). By believing that message, we have received the promised Holy Spirit (Galatians 3:2-5, 14).

LIVING IN FREEDOM

Trusting the good news of Jesus brings freedom, but false Christians wish to enslave us again (Galatians 2:4). In our former lives, we were slaves of sin and prisoners of the law, but now we are free children and heirs of God (Galatians 4:1-31). We should allow no one to enslave us again, but should stand firm in our freedom (Galatians 5:1).

But this freedom does not mean we are free to please ourselves, but free to serve God (Galatians 5:13). Indeed, we have been crucified with Christ so we might live by faith and in freedom.

FREE TO LOVE

Therefore, we are set free from the selfishness of our sinful nature to love God and others. "The only thing that counts is faith expressing itself through love" (Galatians 5:6). The entire law is summed up in the command to love our neighbors as ourselves (Galatians 5:14). That love does not come naturally, but is the fruit of the Holy Spirit at work in us (Galatians 5:22).

So as we read and meditate on Galatians, let us open our hearts to trust the promise of God, the promise that we are his beloved children. Let us live out that faith as free children of God, allowing his Holy Spirit to produce the fruit of love in us each day.

MEDITATIONS ON GALATIANS

THE POPULAR GOSPEL
(GALATIANS 1:1-10)

DAY ONE READING AND QUESTIONS

[1]Paul, an apostle—sent not from men nor by man, but by Jesus Christ and God the Father, who raised him from the dead— [2]and all the brothers with me,

To the churches in Galatia:

1. What is an apostle? How is Paul like and unlike other apostles?

2. What does it mean that Paul is not sent from or by men? Why would Paul begin his letter this way?

3. Why do you think Paul speaks of the resurrection so early in this letter?

DAY TWO READING AND QUESTIONS

[3]Grace and peace to you from God our Father and the Lord Jesus Christ, [4]who gave himself for our sins to rescue us from the present evil age, according to the will of our God and Father, [5]to whom be glory for ever and ever. Amen.

*1. What do the words "grace" and "peace" mean? Why does Paul greet
the Galatians with these words?*

*2. In what ways is the world we live in an evil age? How has Jesus
rescued us from this age?*

*3. What is the will of God in this passage? What do we usually think
of when we talk of the will of God?*

Day Three Reading and Questions

[6]I am astonished that you are so quickly deserting the one who
called you by the grace of Christ and are turning to a different gospel-
[7]which is really no gospel at all. Evidently some people are throwing
you into confusion and are trying to pervert the gospel of Christ.

*1. Why does the behavior of the Galatians astonish Paul? What does
that tell us about the relationship between Paul and the Galatians?*

*2. Why is a different gospel really no gospel at all? What does "gospel"
mean?*

*3. Why do you think the Galatians are confused about the gospel?
What could have kept them from such confusion?*

Day Four Reading and Questions

[8]But even if we or an angel from heaven should preach a gospel other
than the one we preached to you, let him be eternally condemned! [9]As
we have already said, so now I say again: If anybody is preaching to

you a gospel other than what you accepted, let him be eternally condemned!

[10]Am I now trying to win the approval of men, or of God? Or am I trying to please men? If I were still trying to please men, I would not be a servant of Christ.

> *1. Does Paul really expect an angel to preach another gospel? If not, what is his point in mentioning angels?*

> *2. Isn't it harsh to proclaim people eternally condemned? Why is Paul so harsh?*

> *3. Shouldn't we try to please as many people as possible? Why doesn't Paul want human approval?*

Day Five Reading and Questions

Go back and read the entire passage.

> *1. Have you even been astonished by the behavior of other Christians? Give examples. Do you think those who taught you the gospel might sometimes be astonished at your actions?*

> *2. What "other gospels" challenge believers today? How are they really not gospels at all?*

> *3. Do Christians and churches today sometimes try to hard to please people? If so, why?*

MEDITATION ON GALATIANS 1:1-10

Why would anyone leave "good news" behind? Why would anyone desert the grace of Christ for something else?

No wonder Paul was astonished at the Galatians.

But two thousand years later, are we contemporary Christians any different? "Of course we are," some might say. "We would never abandon the gospel!"

Yet many "advanced" versions of the good news entice us today. Several famous Christian teachers with enormous followings promise health, wealth, success, happy families, a strong country, and comfortable lives to those who follow their version of the gospel.

Jesus, however, promised suffering. "Take up the cross daily." Paul spread that message. "We must go through many hardships to enter the kingdom of God" (Acts 14:22).

The different gospel the Galatians followed promised assurance based on performance of the law and circumcision. The different gospel today promises assurance based on ease of life. Both are different gospels. Both are no gospels at all.

But why would anyone follow counterfeit gospels? Paul gives a hint in the last verse of this passage. Paul is pleasing God, not people. Paul's good news from Jesus is not designed to make him or his message popular. The message of Jesus was so unpopular it cost him his life. Paul's gospel cost him. Like Jesus, he also knew suffering and death.

We live in an age where truth is measured by popularity, where politicians rule by poll numbers, and where even spirituality must be quantified. It takes great courage to stay with the original gospel and to resist the urge to please people. Only the continuing grace of God can give us that courage.

Would Paul be astonished at us? Is Jesus disappointed in us? Are we trying our best to please as many people as possible or are we servants of Christ?

"Lord Jesus, may you truly be our Lord. Keep us from the lordship of popularity and approval. May we this day live out the good news by taking up our crosses."

FROM JESUS, NOT HUMANS

(GALATIANS 1:11-2:10)

Day One Reading and Questions

[11]I want you to know, brothers, that the gospel I preached is not something that man made up. [12]I did not receive it from any man, nor was I taught it; rather, I received it by revelation from Jesus Christ.

[13]For you have heard of my previous way of life in Judaism, how intensely I persecuted the church of God and tried to destroy it. [14]I was advancing in Judaism beyond many Jews of my own age and was extremely zealous for the traditions of my fathers. [15]But when God, who set me apart from birth and called me by his grace, was pleased [16]to reveal his Son in me so that I might preach him among the Gentiles, I did not consult any man, [17]nor did I go up to Jerusalem to see those who were apostles before I was, but I went immediately into Arabia and later returned to Damascus.

1. *Why is it so important to Paul that he was not taught the gospel by human beings? What would have been so wrong with his learning the gospel from others?*

2. *Why does Paul mention his "previous way of life" here? Is he proud of that former life?*

3. *What is the significance of Paul not going to Jerusalem to see the apostles after his conversion?*

Day Two Reading and Questions

[18]Then after three years, I went up to Jerusalem to get acquainted with Peter and stayed with him fifteen days. [19]I saw none of the other apostles—only James, the Lord's brother. [20]I assure you before God that what I am writing you is no lie. [21]Later I went to Syria and Cilicia. [22]I was personally unknown to the churches of Judea that are in Christ. [23]They only heard the report: "The man who formerly persecuted us is now preaching the faith he once tried to destroy." [24]And they praised God because of me.

1. *Why do you think Paul wanted to get acquainted with Peter? What are some things you think they discussed?*

2. *Why does Paul assure his readers he is not lying? Is someone accusing him of lying?*

3. *Why would the Judean churches praise God because of Paul? Did Paul seek that praise?*

Day Three Reading and Questions

[1]Fourteen years later I went up again to Jerusalem, this time with Barnabas. I took Titus along also. [2]I went in response to a revelation and set before them the gospel that I preach among the Gentiles. But I did this privately to those who seemed to be leaders, for fear that I was running or had run my race in vain. [3]Yet not even Titus, who was with me, was compelled to be circumcised, even though he was a Greek. [4]This matter arose because some false brothers had infiltrated our ranks to spy on the freedom we have in Christ Jesus and to make us

slaves. [5]We did not give in to them for a moment, so that the truth of the gospel might remain with you.

> 1. *Why was it important for Paul to say he went to Jerusalem "in response to a revelation"?*

> 2. *Have you ever known "false brothers" who spy on other Christians? What motivates them? Why is this behavior so offensive?*

> 3. *When is it right to give in to others? When should we not "give in to them for a moment"?*

Day Four Reading and Questions

[6]As for those who seemed to be important—whatever they were makes no difference to me; God does not judge by external appearance—those men added nothing to my message. [7]On the contrary, they saw that I had been entrusted with the task of preaching the gospel to the Gentiles, just as Peter had been to the Jews. [8]For God, who was at work in the ministry of Peter as an apostle to the Jews, was also at work in my ministry as an apostle to the Gentiles. [9]James, Peter and John, those reputed to be pillars, gave me and Barnabas the right hand of fellowship when they recognized the grace given to me. They agreed that we should go to the Gentiles, and they to the Jews. [10]All they asked was that we should continue to remember the poor, the very thing I was eager to do.

> 1. *Who "seemed to be important"? Are these apostles? Why does Paul stress that they added nothing to his message? Is Paul separating himself from the other apostles?*

2. *Who is really at work in the ministry of Peter and Paul? Why is that important to remember?*

3. *What is the "right hand of fellowship"? Is this more than a handshake? What does it imply?*

DAY FIVE READING AND QUESTIONS

Go back and read the entire passage.

1. *What place does "revelation" play in this passage? Who is doing the revealing?*

2. *If Paul learned his gospel from others, what might that imply? Is Paul a second-class apostle because he was not one of the original twelve? What difference would it make to the Galatians if Paul were not an apostle?*

3. *What would have happened if Paul had circumcised Titus? Why is this such a big deal?*

MEDITATION ON GALATIANS 1:11-2:10

False brothers and sisters.

After all that Paul had been through for the cause of Christ—beatings, shipwrecks, and other hardships—perhaps nothing was so trying to his faith as false brothers and sisters.

Is it the same with us? We can take the jeering of outsiders. We are not surprised that the world hates us. But we are surprised when those who claim to be our brothers and sisters in Christ turn against us, lie about us, spy on us, and restrict our freedom in Christ.

How should we react to false brothers and sisters? With anger? Perhaps, to some extent. Paul is angry in this letter of Galatians, particularly angry at the influence these false Christians have on the Galatians. They have led them to a false gospel!

Do we react with fear? Do we try to please the false brothers and sisters? Do we give in to them so no one will be offended? Absolutely not! Paul does not give in to them for a moment. This is not stubbornness on Paul's part; after all, this is the same Paul who wants to be all things to all people for the sake of the gospel. Instead, this is a refusal to allow anyone to undermine the good news of Jesus, the news that brings freedom.

So how should we react to false brothers and sisters who stab us in the back? With grace? Certainly. Forgiveness? Of course. But we do not let them lead others away from the true grace of God. We react, like Paul, by focusing on what really matters. Not on who is right and who is wrong, but on the true source of the gospel. This is not a human message. It comes from God alone. This is not Paul's opinion or our opinion or the opinion of others (even apostles or angels). It is the work of God in Paul, in Peter, in us.

We dare not let the hurt we feel toward false brothers and sisters blind us to the powerful work of God who reveals himself to us and to all in Jesus Christ.

"Father, give us strength to love even our brothers and sisters who turn against us. Give us courage to not give in to those who would turn your freedom into slavery."

HYPOCRISY

(GALATIANS 2:11-3:14)

Day One Reading and Questions

[11]When Peter came to Antioch, I opposed him to his face, because he was clearly in the wrong. [12]Before certain men came from James, he used to eat with the Gentiles. But when they arrived, he began to draw back and separate himself from the Gentiles because he was afraid of those who belonged to the circumcision group. [13]The other Jews joined him in his hypocrisy, so that by their hypocrisy even Barnabas was led astray.

[14]When I saw that they were not acting in line with the truth of the gospel, I said to Peter in front of them all, "You are a Jew, yet you live like a Gentile and not like a Jew. How is it, then, that you force Gentiles to follow Jewish customs?

1. *What caused Peter to stop eating with the Gentiles? Does that same emotion cause us to withdraw from certain people today? Should it?*

2. *Is it ever right to confront fellow Christian about their behavior? If so, what keeps us from those confrontations? What might lead us to confront others more often?*

3. *How are Peter's actions hypocrisy? What is hypocrisy? Is this the usual way hypocrites act?*

Day Two Reading and Questions

[15]"We who are Jews by birth and not 'Gentile sinners' [16]know that a man is not justified by observing the law, but by faith in Jesus Christ. So we, too, have put our faith in Christ Jesus that we may be justified by faith in Christ and not by observing the law, because by observing the law no one will be justified.

[17]"If, while we seek to be justified in Christ, it becomes evident that we ourselves are sinners, does that mean that Christ promotes sin? Absolutely not! [18]If I rebuild what I destroyed, I prove that I am a lawbreaker. [19]For through the law I died to the law so that I might live for God. [20]I have been crucified with Christ and I no longer live, but Christ lives in me. The life I live in the body, I live by faith in the Son of God, who loved me and gave himself for me. [21]I do not set aside the grace of God, for if righteousness could be gained through the law, Christ died for nothing!"

1. *Paul here admits he is a lawbreaker. How can he be a lawbreaker and still be justified? Are we right with God even when we break the law? If so, how?*

2. *"I have been crucified with Christ and I no longer live, but Christ lives in me." This is a famous statement that we often take out of context. How does it fit with the story of Peter told above? What does it have to do with the law?*

3. *If we are not saved by keeping law, what role does obedience have in the life of Christians? Who is it we live for?*

Day Three Reading and Questions

[1]You foolish Galatians! Who has bewitched you? Before your very eyes Jesus Christ was clearly portrayed as crucified. [2]I would like to learn just one thing from you: Did you receive the Spirit by observing the law, or by believing what you heard? [3]Are you so foolish? After beginning with the Spirit, are you now trying to attain your goal by human effort? [4]Have you suffered so much for nothing—if it really was for nothing? [5]Does God give you his Spirit and work miracles among you because you observe the law, or because you believe what you heard?

1. *Paul here reminds the Galatians of their experience of the Holy Spirit. What role does experience play in the life of Christians? Should we emphasize our religious experience more or less than we do?*

2. *Discuss some ways we as Christians can begin with the Spirit and then rely on our own effort to gain salvation.*

3. *Besides their Spirit experience, Paul mentions their experience of suffering. What role does suffering play in our walk with God?*

Day Four Reading and Questions

[6]Consider Abraham: "He believed God, and it was credited to him as righteousness." [7]Understand, then, that those who believe are children of Abraham. [8]The Scripture foresaw that God would justify the Gentiles by faith, and announced the gospel in advance to Abraham: "All nations will be blessed through you." [9]So those who have faith are blessed along with Abraham, the man of faith.

[10]All who rely on observing the law are under a curse, for it is written: "Cursed is everyone who does not continue to do everything written in the Book of the Law." [11]Clearly no one is justified before God by the law, because, "The righteous will live by faith." [12]The law is not based on faith; on the contrary, "The man who does these things will live by them." [13]Christ redeemed us from the curse of the law by becoming a curse for us, for it is written: "Cursed is everyone who is hung on a tree." [14]He redeemed us in order that the blessing given to Abraham might come to the Gentiles through Christ Jesus, so that by faith we might receive the promise of the Spirit.

1. *Why is it important to be a child of Abraham? How are Gentiles (those not physically descended from Abraham) made children of Abraham?*

2. *How many sins does one have to commit to be cursed by the law? How did Christ take that curse away?*

3. *List all the things faith does for us in these verses. What does "faith" mean here?*

Day Five Reading and Questions

Go back and read the entire passage.

1. *How did Peter's action contradict the idea that we are saved by faith not by observing the law? How do people today contradict the gospel that salvation is by faith?*

2. *What place does the cross play in these verses? What is accomplished by the crucifixion?*

3. If we really believe that we are saved by trusting Jesus, how does that affect how we treat others?

MEDITATION ON GALATIANS 2:11-3:14

We are saved by faith. Every Christian knows this. It is by trusting in the cross of Christ that we are made right with God.

But do we live that way? That's the question Peter faced. Certainly, Peter knew that we are saved by faith. He knew it. He experienced it. He preached it. But he didn't always live it. Out of fear of what others would think of him, he refused to eat with those who did not keep all of God's laws.

Wasn't Peter just being smart? Wasn't he trying not to offend Jewish believers? Wasn't he simply compromising to keep the peace?

No! He was forsaking the gospel. So Paul confronts him about his hypocrisy. Peter preaches one way ("By faith we are saved!") but lives another (faith is not enough for me to eat with you).

Do we live by faith? That's the question. "Of course we do," you say. We are a grace church, a faith church. So what do we do with those who want to restrict our freedom in Christ? What do we do with those who say faith is great but it's not enough. We have to keep God's law, too. What do we do when some powerful, long-time members of our church do not approve of the recent "sinners" who have joined us? Out of fear of what they might think, do we draw back and separate ourselves from "sinners" who are saved by the grace of God through faith?

God forbids. This is hypocrisy. If we proclaim faith, we have to accept all who come to Jesus in faith, even if they don't keep laws we think are important.

Why? Because we have been crucified with Christ. Why? Because we have experienced the Holy Spirit. Why? Because this is how God has always dealt with his people from Abraham to us. Faith is tested when we have to accept those who do not keep God's rules exactly the way we do. We accept them not because they are "right" or "wrong" about the law, but because they trust Jesus for salvation. We accept them because God accepts them. We accept, and eat, and live with them because no one keeps the law completely. Not even us. We too are sinners made right by the cross through faith.

"Lord Jesus, forgive our hypocrisy of judging fellow believers because they are not like us. Increase our faith so we may truly love all as you love."

CHILDREN AND HEIRS

(GALATIANS 3:15-4:7)

Day One Reading and Questions

[15]Brothers, let me take an example from everyday life. Just as no one can set aside or add to a human covenant that has been duly established, so it is in this case. [16]The promises were spoken to Abraham and to his seed. The Scripture does not say "and to seeds," meaning many people, but "and to your seed," meaning one person, who is Christ. [17]What I mean is this: The law, introduced 430 years later, does not set aside the covenant previously established by God and thus do away with the promise. [18]For if the inheritance depends on the law, then it no longer depends on a promise; but God in his grace gave it to Abraham through a promise.

1. *Substitute "Will" (as in Last Will and Testament) for "covenant" in these verses. We do not allow a valid Will to be set aside. Does that make this illustration clearer?*

2. *Why is it important that Abraham came before the law?*

3. *What is the contrast here between law and promise? What does each word imply about the way one receives salvation?*

Day Two Reading and Questions

[19]What, then, was the purpose of the law? It was added because of transgressions until the Seed to whom the promise referred had come. The law was put into effect through angels by a mediator. [20]A mediator, however, does not represent just one party; but God is one.

[21]Is the law, therefore, opposed to the promises of God? Absolutely not! For if a law had been given that could impart life, then righteousness would certainly have come by the law. [22]But the Scripture declares that the whole world is a prisoner of sin, so that what was promised, being given through faith in Jesus Christ, might be given to those who believe.

[23]Before this faith came, we were held prisoners by the law, locked up until faith should be revealed. [24]So the law was put in charge to lead us to Christ that we might be justified by faith. [25]Now that faith has come, we are no longer under the supervision of the law.

1. What three things does the law do, according to these verses?

2. Doesn't it sound as though the law opposes the promises of God? What is the relationship between law and promise?

3. How do some Christians today show that they prefer law to promises? Why would anyone prefer law? What is difficult about being saved by promises?

Day Three Reading and Questions

[26]You are all sons of God through faith in Christ Jesus, [27]for all of you who were baptized into Christ have clothed yourselves with

Christ. [28]There is neither Jew nor Greek, slave nor free, male nor female, for you are all one in Christ Jesus. [29]If you belong to Christ, then you are Abraham's seed, and heirs according to the promise.

> *1. What is the relationship between faith and baptism in this passage?*

> *2. What does it mean to clothe ourselves with Christ?*

> *3. In what ways do the distinctions Paul lists-Jew, Greek, slave, free, male, female—disappear in Christ? What implications does this have for the way we do church?*

DAY FOUR READING AND QUESTIONS

[1]What I am saying is that as long as the heir is a child, he is no different from a slave, although he owns the whole estate. [2]He is subject to guardians and trustees until the time set by his father. [3]So also, when we were children, we were in slavery under the basic principles of the world. [4]But when the time had fully come, God sent his Son, born of a woman, born under law, [5]to redeem those under law, that we might receive the full rights of sons. [6]Because you are sons, God sent the Spirit of his Son into our hearts, the Spirit who calls out, "Abba, Father." [7]So you are no longer a slave, but a son; and since you are a son, God has made you also an heir.

> *1. In what sense were we slaves before Jesus came? To whom were we slaves? Explain.*

> *2. "Abba" is the name Jesus used for the Father. What does it mean that we call him by the same name? How are Father, Son, and Spirit related in this passage?*

3. What does it mean to be an heir of God? What does God own? What do his children own?

DAY FIVE READING AND QUESTIONS

Go back and read the entire passage.

1. Do we ever feel that some Christians are not as important as others? Who? Why?

2. Don't most churches have a "core group" of members who do most of the work? Are they not more important than the others in the church?

3. Aren't some Christians more spiritual and more righteous than others?

MEDITATION ON GALATIANS 3:15-4:7

No second-class Christians. No superior Christians.

This is the message of the gospel. We are all one in Christ. We are all children of God. We are all heirs. We all call God, "Abba," Father.

But through the ages and even today, some claim to be superior Christians who look down on other groups as second-class brothers and sisters. The groupings haven't changed much since Paul's day. We don't have slaves in our churches, but some who are "masters," who are professionals or who own their own businesses, look down on the poorer, working class Christians. They forget that if God prefers anyone in Scripture, he prefers the poor. In Christ, the poor are fully heirs, beloved children, not second-class.

Some male Christians think they are superior to female Christians. Sexism is still with us, especially in church. This is not to say that men and women are the same; of course, there are differences. But there is no superiority or inferiority. Women are fully heirs, fully children, completely "in Christ."

What about Jew and Greek? Since Paul's day, the situation may be reversed. Some look down on Jews. But in Christ, all races become one—the new human race begun by Jesus, the race of the baptized.

But more may be going on in the "Jew-Greek" example. The Jews who followed Jesus as the Messiah may have thought themselves superior to Greeks who came out of paganism. Those Jewish Christians could brag about following the law all their lives. But the law simply imprisoned them, because they could not perfectly keep it. The law was to lead them to Christ. The law was preceded by the promise. And promises must be trusted.

As followers of Jesus, we dare not look down on the poor, on women, or on any racial group. What's more, we dare not think ourselves superior because we sin less than others or know the Bible more than others, or commit only socially acceptable sins. None of us deserves to be God's children. All of us (even the "worst") are made children and heirs through Jesus. All we have to do is trust that promise. In that trust, all stand equal under the cross of Christ.

"Lord Jesus, forgive us when we feel superior to fellow believers in any way. May we trust your promise for us and for others. Thank you for bringing us to our "Abba."

SLAVE OR FREE?

(GALATIANS 4:8-5:1)

DAY ONE READING AND QUESTIONS

[8]Formerly, when you did not know God, you were slaves to those who by nature are not gods. [9]But now that you know God—or rather are known by God—how is it that you are turning back to those weak and miserable principles? Do you wish to be enslaved by them all over again? [10]You are observing special days and months and seasons and years! [11]I fear for you, that somehow I have wasted my efforts on you. [12]I plead with you, brothers, become like me, for I became like you. You have done me no wrong. [13]As you know, it was because of an illness that I first preached the gospel to you. [14]Even though my illness was a trial to you, you did not treat me with contempt or scorn. Instead, you welcomed me as if I were an angel of God, as if I were Christ Jesus himself. [15]What has happened to all your joy? I can testify that, if you could have done so, you would have torn out your eyes and given them to me. [16]Have I now become your enemy by telling you the truth?

1. *What are some things that enslaved us before we became Christians? Are we in danger (like the Galatians) of turning back to that slavery? How?*

2. *Do we welcome those who teach us the gospel as we would welcome angels or Jesus himself? Should we? What would that look like?*

3. What attitudes or events threaten to rob us of our joy in Christ?

Day Two Reading and Questions

[17]Those people are zealous to win you over, but for no good. What they want is to alienate you from us, so that you may be zealous for them. [18]It is fine to be zealous, provided the purpose is good, and to be so always and not just when I am with you. [19]My dear children, for whom I am again in the pains of childbirth until Christ is formed in you, [20]how I wish I could be with you now and change my tone, because I am perplexed about you!

1. What does it mean to be zealous? Is it always good to be zealous?

2. Paul compares himself to a mother giving birth. What does this say about his attitude toward the Galatians. Besides your own children, are there others you have given birth to in Christ? How do you feel about them?

3. Name some fellow Christians who perplex you. What should you do about that?

Day Three Reading and Questions

[21]Tell me, you who want to be under the law, are you not aware of what the law says? [22]For it is written that Abraham had two sons, one by the slave woman and the other by the free woman. [23]His son by the slave woman was born in the ordinary way; but his son by the free woman was born as the result of a promise.

[24]These things may be taken figuratively, for the women represent

two covenants. One covenant is from Mount Sinai and bears children who are to be slaves: This is Hagar. [25]Now Hagar stands for Mount Sinai in Arabia and corresponds to the present city of Jerusalem, because she is in slavery with her children. [26]But the Jerusalem that is above is free, and she is our mother. [27]For it is written:

"Be glad, O barren woman,
who bears no children;
break forth and cry aloud,
you who have no labor pains;
because more are the children of the desolate woman
than of her who has a husband."

   1. *Read the Hagar and Sarah story in Genesis 16. What is Paul's point in mentioning this story?*

   2. *What comes to mind when you think of Mt. Sinai? What is the "Jerusalem that is above"?*

   3. *What is the point of the poem on barrenness?*

DAY FOUR READING AND QUESTIONS

[28]Now you, brothers, like Isaac, are children of promise. [29]At that time the son born in the ordinary way persecuted the son born by the power of the Spirit. It is the same now. [30]But what does the Scripture say? "Get rid of the slave woman and her son, for the slave woman's son will never share in the inheritance with the free woman's son." [31]Therefore, brothers, we are not children of the slave woman, but of the free woman.

[1]It is for freedom that Christ has set us free. Stand firm, then, and do not let yourselves be burdened again by a yoke of slavery.

1. What does it mean to be children of promise?

2. Here Isaac is called "one born by the power of the Spirit." How are we like Isaac?

3. What does it mean to be children of the free woman?

DAY FIVE READING AND QUESTIONS

Go back and read the entire passage.

1. How is the concept of slavery used in these verses? What point is Paul making to the Galatians and to us?

2. Why is freedom so important in this passage?

3. What is the relation among freedom, promise, and being God's children?

MEDITATION ON GALATIANS 4:8-5:1

Slave. I cannot imagine what it would be like to be a slave. Can you? To have no rights, no choices, no hope.

Or perhaps we can imagine. We all have been trapped, enslaved, in jobs we cannot stand but feel we must keep. We've been enslaved in relationships we cannot break. We have felt the slavery of addictions we are powerless to overcome.

We were slaves to sin. Slaves to other gods, perhaps not made of stone, but made of money, power, pleasure, and success.

Christ has set us free! That is the heart of the good news of Jesus. Free from sin. Free from the gods of this world. Free from the miserable principles that once ruled our lives. Free to be children and heirs of God.

Shall we live as free people? Or will we fall back into slavery? What a tragedy, to be freed from slavery only to voluntarily return! How? By becoming slaves to human rules and laws, loaded on our backs by false Christians who want to turn our freedom into slavery, all in the name of being strict Christians.

Do we know Christians who are burdened by their walk with God, who constantly feel they are not doing enough for the Lord? Are we one of those Christians, never fully trusting the promise of salvation?

Grasp your freedom! Cast off your chains! Live free, as children of God!

"Holy Father, you have set us free through Christ. Give us the faith to live free and let no one enslave us again."

ACTS OR FRUIT?

(GALATIANS 5:2-26)

Day One Reading and Questions

[2]Mark my words! I, Paul, tell you that if you let yourselves be circumcised, Christ will be of no value to you at all. [3]Again I declare to every man who lets himself be circumcised that he is obligated to obey the whole law. [4]You who are trying to be justified by law have been alienated from Christ; you have fallen away from grace. [5]But by faith we eagerly await through the Spirit the righteousness for which we hope. [6]For in Christ Jesus neither circumcision nor uncircumcision has any value. The only thing that counts is faith expressing itself through love.

[7]You were running a good race. Who cut in on you and kept you from obeying the truth? [8]That kind of persuasion does not come from the one who calls you. [9]"A little yeast works through the whole batch of dough." [10]I am confident in the Lord that you will take no other view. The one who is throwing you into confusion will pay the penalty, whoever he may be. [11]Brothers, if I am still preaching circumcision, why am I still being persecuted? In that case the offense of the cross has been abolished. [12]As for those agitators, I wish they would go the whole way and emasculate themselves!

1. Why is Paul so adamantly against circumcision here? What would it mean for these Gentiles to let themselves be circumcised?

2. Briefly explain the race and yeast examples Paul gives here. What point is he making?

3. What is the offense of the cross? How would preaching circumcision abolish that offense? Should we do away with the offense of the cross?

DAY TWO READING AND QUESTIONS

[13]You, my brothers, were called to be free. But do not use your freedom to indulge the sinful nature; rather, serve one another in love. [14]The entire law is summed up in a single command: "Love your neighbor as yourself." [15]If you keep on biting and devouring each other, watch out or you will be destroyed by each other.

[16]So I say, live by the Spirit, and you will not gratify the desires of the sinful nature. [17]For the sinful nature desires what is contrary to the Spirit, and the Spirit what is contrary to the sinful nature. They are in conflict with each other, so that you do not do what you want. [18]But if you are led by the Spirit, you are not under law.

1. How can freedom be abused? Does being free in Christ mean we can do anything we please? What limits freedom?

2. Describe the "sinful nature" (some translations call this "the flesh"). Is this the body? Or is it some inward principle or motivation?

3. What does it mean to be led by the Spirit?

DAY THREE READING AND QUESTIONS

[19]The acts of the sinful nature are obvious: sexual immorality, impurity and debauchery; [20]idolatry and witchcraft; hatred, discord, jealousy, fits of rage, selfish ambition, dissensions, factions [21]and envy; drunkenness, orgies, and the like. I warn you, as I did before, that those who live like this will not inherit the kingdom of God.

1. These acts are grouped in four categories separated by semicolons. How would you describe the basic sin in each category?

2. What surprises you on this list? What act does not seem as bad as others on the list? What do you think is the worst act?

3. Paul has said we are not made right with God through law. Aren't these laws? Isn't Paul prohibiting these actions? Are we right with God by avoiding these acts?

DAY FOUR READING AND QUESTIONS

[22]But the fruit of the Spirit is love, joy, peace, patience, kindness, goodness, faithfulness, [23]gentleness and self-control. Against such things there is no law. [24]Those who belong to Christ Jesus have crucified the sinful nature with its passions and desires. [25]Since we live by the Spirit, let us keep in step with the Spirit. [26]Let us not become conceited, provoking and envying each other.

1. Are these virtues than anyone can have? Or is the fruit of the Spirit different? For example, is the "love" listed here different from ordinary human love?

2. Why does Paul say there is no law against these things? Isn't that obvious? How does this relate to his use of "law" elsewhere in Galatians?

3. Why does Paul warn against conceit here? If we have these virtues, might we become conceited? What keeps us from it?

DAY FIVE READING AND QUESTIONS

Go back and read the entire passage.

1. We often study the acts of the sinful nature and the fruit of the Spirit apart from their context in Galatians. How do they relate to the larger message of Galatians about promises, faith, and freedom?

2. What does Paul say about love in this passage?

3. Paul discusses the "acts" of the sinful nature but the "fruit" of the Spirit. What do these two terms imply?

MEDITATION ON GALATIANS 5:2-26

Love is what matters. Or as this reading says, "The only thing that counts is faith expressing itself through love."

No one can disagree with that. We are all for love. But, how does that trusting love express itself? What does it look like?

It is no ordinary human love. It is more than the most extraordinary human love. It is a supernatural love, from God himself. It is the fruit of the Spirit. This love can be described in other ways: joy, peace, patience, kindness, goodness, faithfulness, gentleness and self-control. Again, these are not virtues we create or pursue. They are the super- natural fruit of the Spirit in us.

So there are two ways. There is the "natural" way of living. Looking out for ourselves. Living for pleasure. Fighting with others over who has the power. Manipulating others, even the gods of this age, for our own success. Keeping God's law to be superior to others. At one level, all of this comes naturally to us.

And there is the spiritual, supernatural way of life. We open our- selves to the love of God, trusting that he has made us right with him in Christ. We open our hearts to the love of God he has poured out on us through his Spirit. We follow the lead of the Spirit, day by day and step by step. Here there is no place for superiority, for boasting, for conceit. All is a gift. All is fruit from the garden of the Lord.

"Father, keep me from the life that comes so easy to me—selfish- ness, envy, and fighting. Open my heart to your Spirit. Guide my feet to keep in step with your love."

NEW CREATION

(GALATIANS 6:1-18)

Day One Reading and Questions

[1]Brothers, if someone is caught in a sin, you who are spiritual should restore him gently. But watch yourself, or you also may be tempted. [2]Carry each other's burdens, and in this way you will fulfill the law of Christ. [3]If anyone thinks he is something when he is nothing, he deceives himself. [4]Each one should test his own actions. Then he can take pride in himself, without comparing himself to somebody else, [5]for each one should carry his own load.

1. What does "caught" in a sin imply?

2. Why is there a warning against pride in this passage?

3. We are told here to carry each other's burdens and to carry our own load. How can both be true?

Day Two Reading and Questions

[6]Anyone who receives instruction in the word must share all good things with his instructor.
[7]Do not be deceived: God cannot be mocked. A man reaps what

he sows. [8]The one who sows to please his sinful nature, from that nature will reap destruction; the one who sows to please the Spirit, from the Spirit will reap eternal life.

1. *Since Paul himself often preached without pay, why does he encourage them to share with their instructors? Is it important to pay preachers? Why?*

2. *You reap what you sow. Does this teaching contradict the emphasis on freedom and grace in Galatians?*

3. *What does it mean to sow to please the Spirit?*

DAY THREE READING AND QUESTIONS

[9]Let us not become weary in doing good, for at the proper time we will reap a harvest if we do not give up. [10]Therefore, as we have opportunity, let us do good to all people, especially to those who belong to the family of believers.

1. *What makes us burn out in doing good? What can keep us from such burnout?*

2. *Why should we especially do good to the family of believers? Doesn't this sound selfish? Shouldn't we care more for those outside the church?*

3. *We should do good to reap a harvest. What is this harvest? Is it more than heavenly reward?*

Day Four Reading and Questions

[11]See what large letters I use as I write to you with my own hand! [12]Those who want to make a good impression outwardly are trying to compel you to be circumcised. The only reason they do this is to avoid being persecuted for the cross of Christ. [13]Not even those who are circumcised obey the law, yet they want you to be circumcised that they may boast about your flesh. [14]May I never boast except in the cross of our Lord Jesus Christ, through which the world has been crucified to me, and I to the world. [15]Neither circumcision nor uncircumcision means anything; what counts is a new creation. [16]Peace and mercy to all who follow this rule, even to the Israel of God.

[17]Finally, let no one cause me trouble, for I bear on my body the marks of Jesus.

[18]The grace of our Lord Jesus Christ be with your spirit, brothers. Amen.

1. *Paul says some were being circumcised to avoid persecution. What are some things we do today to avoid persecution?*

2. *We should boast only in the cross. What does that mean? What are other religious acts that we might be tempted to boast about?*

3. *Paul talks about following a rule and being the Israel of God. Is he talking only to Jews? If not, how are we the Israel of God?*

Day Five Reading and Questions

Go back and read the entire passage.

1. Paul strongly says we are saved by a promise, not by keeping the law. Yet here he just as strongly condemns sin. What keeps us most from sin, following law or trusting the promise? How does that work?

2. We are told here to do good works. What is our motivation for good works? Do we do them to be saved?

3. What is the new creation? How does it relate to sin and the sinful nature? How does it relate to persecution? To pleasing the Spirit?

MEDITATION ON GALATIANS 6:1-18

A new creation. What does it mean?

It means looking out for others, not ourselves. It means correcting and forgiving others their faults without any thought of superiority on our part. It means shouldering their load as well as our own.

The new creation works like the old. You reap what you sow. However in the new creation this is not simply getting what you deserve. Thank God, he does not give us what we deserve! Instead, it means living to please the Spirit, the Holy Spirit of God who gives life to the new creation.

New creation also means suffering and persecution. It is not taking the easy way out by keeping rules just to make others happy. It is boasting not in what we have accomplished, but in the cross of Christ, the cross whose sufferings we share.

We are left with a choice. We can go back to being ruled by our sinful nature. We can desert the gospel for another, one that falsely promises a higher spirituality and a stricter righteousness. We can be proud of our obedience and look down on those less spiritual than we are. We can grow tired of doing good. That is the old creation. That is the false gospel.

Or we can trust the promises of God. We can love one another and do good to one another without bragging. We can embrace the cross of Christ. We can be crucified to the world. We can live in the new creation and reap eternal life.

"Father, keep us from the false gospel. Guard us against pride. Give us courage to embrace the persecution of the cross that leads to eternal life. Give us your Holy Spirit."

A companion volume by the same author

Living God's Love:
An Invitation to Christian Spirituality

176 pages, $12.99 • ISBN 0-9748441-2-8

by Gary Holloway & Earl Lavender

A simple, practical introduction
to the classic spiritual disciplines.
A wonderful tool for study groups,
prayer groups, and classes.

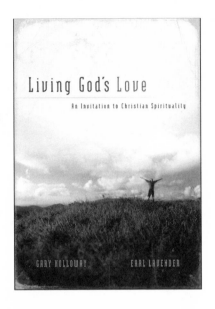

"Our world is hungry for a life-giving way of life. That is what
Jesus offered—and offers still. Living God's Love *makes that way*
real and alive and accessible to real-world people."

JOHN ORTBERG, AUTHOR OF *THE LIFE YOU'VE ALWAYS WANTED*

"At last: a book that brings the essential subject of spiritual formation down
to earth. Clear, reverent, practical, and warm—I'll give this book to people in
my church to help them get on a healthy path of authentic Christian living."

BRIAN MCLAREN, AUTHOR OF *A NEW KIND OF CHRISTIAN*

 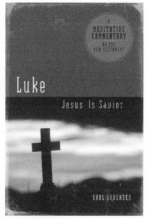 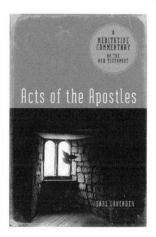
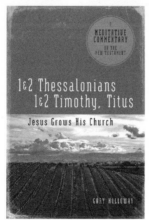

NOTES